Wisdom From Ancient Greek Philosophy:

UNCOVERING STOICISM AND A DAILY

STOIC JOURNAL

George Tanner

© 2018

THIS COLLECTION INCLUDES THE FOLLOWING BOOKS:

<u>Stoicism: Learn A Detailed Breakdown on Stoicism Philosophy and Wisdom from the Greats</u>

AND

<u>Daily Stoic A Daily Journal: On Meditation, Stoicism, Wisdom and Philosophy, to Improve your Life</u>

COPYRIGHT

Stoicism: Learn A Detailed Breakdown on Stoicism Philosophy and Wisdom from the Greats

Daily Stoic A Daily Journal: On Meditation, Stoicism, Wisdom and Philosophy, to Improve your Life

By George Tanner

Copyright @2018 By George Tanner

All Rights Reserved.

The following eBook is reproduced below with the goal of providing information that is as accurate and as reliable as possible. Regardless, purchasing this eBook can be seen as consent to the fact that both the publisher and the author of this book are in no way experts on the topics discussed within, and that any recommendations or suggestions made herein are for entertainment purposes only. Professionals should be consulted as needed before undertaking any of the action endorsed herein.

This declaration is deemed fair and valid by both the American Bar Association and the Committee of Publishers Association and is legally binding throughout the United States.

Furthermore, the transmission, duplication or reproduction of any of the following work, including precise information, will be considered an illegal act, irrespective whether it is done electronically or in print. The legality extends to creating a secondary or tertiary copy of the work or a recorded copy and is only allowed with express written consent of the Publisher. All additional rights are reserved.

The information in the following pages is broadly considered to be a truthful and accurate account of facts, and as such any inattention, use or misuse of the information in question by the reader will render any resulting actions solely under their purview. There are no scenarios in which the publisher or the original author of this work can be in any fashion deemed liable for any hardship or damages that may befall them after undertaking information described herein.

Additionally, the information found on the following pages is intended for informational purposes only and should thus be considered, universal. As befitting its nature, the information presented is without assurance regarding its continued validity or interim quality. Trademarks that mentioned are done without written consent and can in no way be considered an endorsement from the trademark holder.

Table of Contents

- STOICISM: 1
- INTRODUCTION 1
- HISTORY OF STOICISM 8
- THE GOOD LIFE 21
- ON CONTROL 28
- VIRTUE IN STOICISM 37
- STOIC LOGIC AND YOU 45
- COSMOLOGY AND THEOLOGY IN STOICISM 56
- STOICISM AND PSYCHOLOGY 61
- STOICISM AND THE EMOTIONS 71
- OUTER TROUBLES; PREVENTATIVE MEASURES IN STOICISM 80
- STOIC DISCOMFORT 90
- APATHEIA – STOIC INNER PEACE 97
- CONCLUSION 103
- DESCRIPTION 110

- DAILY STOIC: 113
- DESCRIPTION 113

INTRODUCTION	114
INTRODUCTION: STOICISM AND THE VIRTUOUS LIFE	116
I. WINTER WOES	120
II. SPRING IN BLOOM	158
III. BEAT THE HEAT WITH SUMMER VIRTUE	205
IV. FALL, A TIME OF CHANGE	231
BIBLIOGRAPHY	259

STOICISM:

INTRODUCTION

For over two thousand years the Stoic school has lived, died and been reborn according to the whims of fortune. In its earliest days, it consisted of a small but precocious group of Greeks pacing the public spaces of Athens, teaching virtue by example and challenging vice with argument and irony. In its middle period, it yawned through the Greek islands and into Anatolia and developed a consistent doctrine which earned it a place among the great schools of ancient philosophy. At its height, it stretched across the Mediterranean, carried by the ships and soldiers of the Roman Empire, and whispered in the ears of statesmen and slaves alike. And when its flame was extinguished with the Empire in which it burned, it lived on through Christian doctrine and belief, a specter floating through the pens and consciousnesses of monks and theologians as they copied and recopied texts and carried its ideas into the modern age.

Today it lives again, first and with the great energy in cognitive behavioral therapy, and second in its own right, as a philosophy whose message resonates in spite of its age. Its emphasis on living well, on attention to others, our community, our planet, meet modern problems at the heart and shift the focus of daily life from living well in the sense of pleasure to living well in the sense of virtue. And as a bonus, Stoicism teaches how to deal with difficult coworkers, to cope with stress, to live according to our values, and to choose values that are becoming of our nature as human beings.

So what is Stoicism? The answer to this question in many ways turns on another question: What is wisdom? Further, what part does wisdom play in our daily lives? For the Stoics, wisdom is the virtue that governs all others. It directs us first to choose our ends, those things for the sake of which we do everything else, and how to pursue those ends. If I am a thief and I come up with a new trick or a subtle way of pilfering what does not belong to me, I am clever because I was inventive in obtaining my goal. But I am not wise because my goal, to take what is not mine, is not just, because it damages both the person from whom I am stealing, insofar as I have hurt them materially, and myself, insofar as I have degraded myself by the practice of a vice. Similarly, if I have a noble end, for example dedicating myself to charity, but in order to carry out this end I take loans and bury myself in unsustainable debt, I am not wise because I acted imprudently in pursuit of my goal. Both justice and prudence are cardinal virtues for the Stoics, and they appear together such that it is impossible to practice one while violating another. Stealing from one person in order to be charitable to another, for example, is neither just nor prudent. It is not just because, as before, it is an injury to myself and to another party, and it is not prudent because it is unjust. Stoicism is that school of philosophy for which wisdom, being for them the state that obtains in a fully developed human nature, is the end of all ethical activity, is the goal of practicing the virtues in correct relationship with one another, and is thus the goal of an ethical life.

Stoicism as an ancient school may be thought in opposition to its rivals. Aristotle's Peripatetic school held that the end goal of an ethical life was *eudaimonia*, which roughly translates as human flourishing. Wisdom and the other virtues were and are important for Aristotelian ethics, but, unlike for the Stoics, they were not sufficient for the good life, nor did they exhaust human happiness—pleasure and a bit of good fortune are also necessary on Aristotle's view. For the Epicureans, another rival school, pleasure is the aim of ethical life, is sufficient for a good life, in particular, the relief of pain. More than any other school, the Epicureans were direct competitors with the Stoics. It might be easy to see why. They are, for example, not as concerned with virtue as either the Peripatetics or the Stoics, and though they also hold wisdom to be a cardinal virtue, prudence, for them correct choices with respect to pleasure and pain, is the center of the virtues.

The love of wisdom is, for the Stoics as with their contemporaries, a life in a state of what may be called a kind of desperation. It is akin to a lover who thinks only of their beloved. In his Symposium, Plato has Socrates say that love lives between humans and their desires. The end of love, the result of the lover's union with their beloved, is reproduction. In the case of people, love's aim is the creation of children. In the case of trades, love's aim is the production of crafts. And in the case of wisdom, the lover seeks to produce and to spread concepts. In a sense, then, the philosopher's goal is always pedagogical. Where possible the philosopher seeks out the truth of the world behind appearances. But not satisfied with keeping knowledge, the philosopher endeavors to spread it through thought and action, to right error by example and fill the gaps of discourse.

Stoicism is a life devoted to this pedagogical discipline. It emphasizes practice, living by example, by teaching the doctrines of Stoicism, particularly ethics, and by exemplifying its doctrines. The Stoics collectively characterize philosophy as *askêsis*, a kind of practice of knowledge concerning the beneficial. Their approach to philosophy was therapeutic; their emphasis was developing good habits through knowledge of what is and is not to be valued. They aim to strengthen *prohairesis*, the faculty of choice, and to thereby cultivate wisdom, to become Stoic sages.

Maybe the greatest hurdle to the adoption of Stoic ideas is how few of their works are extant. This is a problem not at all uncommon when interpreting classical thinkers. We have lists of works written by Epicurus, Aristotle and Zeno, provided to us by authors like Diogenes Laertius, very few of which survive, if any. We can nonetheless build accurate, if not always consistent, accounts of what these thinkers say. For the Stoics in particular, our main references are Roman philosophers like Epictetus, Seneca, Plutarch, and Cicero, and, of course, Marcus Aurelius. They preserved the core of Stoicism, and in a way that engages with their peers and draws on a wealth of social and historical examples. It is to these Roman thinkers that I will turn in exploring Stoicism here, and from the examples given at the height of the Roman Empire.

Stoicism's heart and goal is a life in accordance with nature. As Emperor Marcus Aurelius says in book six of his *Meditations*,

"In conformity to the nature of the universe, every single thing is accomplished, for certainly it is not in conformity to any other nature that each thing is accomplished, either a nature which externally comprehends this or a nature which is comprehended within this nature, or a nature external and independent of this."[1]

---

[1]　　Marcus Aurelius, *Meditations,* book six

The Stoic idea of nature is different than the modern idea. Both instinct and inheritance play a role, like our modern concept, but they include the full development of a thing in their conversation. What is the Stoic idea of nature? If I, for example, asked "what is the nature of this seed?" you may answer "to become a tree." Your answer accords with the idea of nature the Stoics employ; the seed's nature is not just an embryo contained in a coat with its nutrients, but also that it will become a tree when conditions pertain. Similarly, an individual may steal, lie, cheat and practice infidelity because of some evolutionary adaptation, and an undeveloped person may have these behaviors as part of their nature, but also part of their nature is the capacity to grow beyond these limits, to become rationally and morally developed. The former is a life of animality for the Stoics. As Epictetus says in book one, chapter six of his *Discourses*,

"What, then, are these things done in us only. Many, indeed, in us only, of which the rational animal had peculiar need; but you will find many common to us with irrational animals. Do they them understand what is done? By no means. For use is one thing, and understanding is another: God had need of irrational animals to make use of appearances, but of us to understand the use of appearances. It is, therefore, enough for them to eat and to drink, and to sleep and to copulate, and to do all the other things which they severally do. But for us, to whom He has given also the faculty, these things are not sufficient; for unless we act in a proper and orderly manner, and conformably to the nature and constitution of each thing, we shall never attain our true end."[2]

If a seed that never becomes a tree can be said to have failed in its nature, so too can a person who never develops morally be said to have failed.

Moral maturity implies a life cultivated by and in virtue. For this reason, the virtues in Stoic doctrine guide action. The cardinal Stoic virtues are courage, temperance, prudence, and justice. Without these, life is animalistic, unworthy of the name "human." There is no easy path or royal road to this life. Stoicism demands a foundation of good habits and a critical disposition. And such a character is precisely what Stoicism aims to cultivate.

---

[2] Epictetus, *Discourses*, book one, chapter six

History of Stoicism

Among the ranks of the Stoics are scientists, craftsmen, merchants, farmers, politicians—people from every corner of society. What brings them together is their commitment to virtue, their common ethical and intellectual origin, and the practice of Stoic living. Stoicism, like other Western traditions, has its origins in Greece. Their founder is Zeno of Citium. Neither his nor the works of his most famous successor of the same period, Chrysippus, survive. Scholars across the ages have nonetheless constructed an account of their lives from testimony and existing evidence. I can, using their conclusions, give a general history of the origins of Stoic philosophy and its development.

Zeno was born in Cyprus the same year Alexander the Great was, around 336 B.C.E. He was the son of a merchant, and himself became a merchant when he was of age. In one account, in his 20s he experienced a tragic shipwreck, which marked the end of his life at sea. On another account, he was already in Athens when he learned that one of his shipments was lost to the waves. On either account, in Athens he was introduced to Xenophon's Memorabilia, and from it the character of Socrates, whom he admired. Later, he studied under Crates of Thebes and Stilpon of Megara, philosophers of the Cynic school (the same school to which Diogenes of Synope belonged). Accounts from

Diogenes Laertius say that he greeted the shipwreck as an act of good fortune because it allowed him to shed his old life and devote himself to the study of philosophy.

Zeno is famous for teaching in the Stoa Poikile or Painted Porch, a central location in Athens where the bounty from distant wars was displayed for the public. It is after this porch that the Stoics would be named, but their original name was the "Zenonians." In the Stoa Poikile, Zeno discussed virtue and its superiority over pleasure and described a natural law which held precedence over the random swerve of atoms. Both the position that pleasure was the good and that randomly moving atoms were the governing principle of the universe was held by the Epicureans. Zeno also lived his teachings, and he was praised throughout his life for his consistency and his prudence.

Zeno lived and taught in Athens for the remainder of his life. His death is said to be akin to that of Diogenes of Sinope. As an old man, after breaking a toe, he declared himself satisfied with the life he had lived and strangled himself to death. The story may be apocryphal, but it exemplifies his strength of will, his good character, and his self-discipline.

Zeno was followed by Cleanthes, son of Phanias, a native of Assos. Diogenes Laertius tells us Cleanthes began life as a pugilist who arrived in Athens with only four drachmas to his name. Upon meeting Zeno, he adopted a life of philosophical study. He was known for being industrious, driven by his extreme poverty to work his entire life. At night he drew water in gardens belonging to the wealthy and by day he exercised his mind via rigorous argumentation. In his time he was known as a second Heracles, a notable Presocratic philosopher, because of his lean and modest lifestyle and his serious temperament. When he could not afford the paper on which to record Zeno's lectures, he is said to instead have used oyster-shells and the bones of oxen. When Zeno died, Cleanthes carried forward the Zenoian tradition in his teaching and writings.

Cleanthes too died when he was ready. He is said to have suffered from inflammation of his gums, perhaps an account of gingivitis, and was advised by his doctors to forego eating for two days. When the treatment proved successful, his doctors told him that he could resume his diet, but Cleanthes refused. According to him, his life had been long enough, and he was content to end it on his terms. He fasted for the remainder of his days until his death and is said to have died at the same age Zeno had before him.

A whole generation after Zeno washed up on the Athenian shore, in 280 B.C.E., Chrysippus of Soli, the third head of the Zenoian school, was born. Diogenes Laertius says Chrysippus' father, Apollonius, left him a fortune, which he later lost defending himself against legal trouble. It was his misfortune which led him to philosophy, as was the case with Zeno.

Chrysippus studied at Plato's Academy and studies physics, rhetoric, and dialectic. He then studied under Cleanthes. When Cleanthes died, Chrysippus inherited Zeno's legacy and became the head of the Stoic school.

In his lifetime Chrysippus wrote over 700 scrolls, none of which survive. In them, he wrote about ethics, physics, logic and argumentation, epistemology and cosmology. He drew extensively from the testimony of other thinkers, so much so that he was often mocked, alleged by his rivals to have nothing of his own to contribute, or that, if his citations were removed from his works, their pages would be blank. His writing style was mirrored in his arguments. It was not seldom that he argued in favor of both positions in a debate and even professed absurd positions if he thought they had pedagogical merit. His students and his opponents alike were baffled and frustrated by his behavior. But we might not find it strange if we remember that Socrates, too, used irony and claimed positions which he did not believe if he thought something could thereby be learned.

Much of what is today called Stoic logic, which we will discuss at length in a later chapter, was developed by Chrysippus. Chrysippus' logic is an ancient alternative to Aristotelian logic and is similar to modern propositional logic pioneered by Gottlob Frege. Chrysippus' logic is at the heart of Stoic advances in science and mathematics, and formalized the notion of "disjunction." Diogenes Laertius noted 118 logical texts penned under Chrysippus' name, seven alone of which tackled the Liar's Paradox. Chrysippus believed that a rigorous ethical system required a foundation in logic and reason, these being the guideposts for everything that exists.

The middle Stoics did not significantly advance the school, so we will only talk briefly about them here. Panaetius, son of Nicagoras, was born almost a century after Chrysippus, in about 180 B.C.E. He studied under Crates of Mallus, a prominent linguist, and then under Critolaus and Carneades before studying under the Stoic philosopher Diogenes of Babylon. His principle work was in ethics, where he argued that physics, not logic, was the starting point of philosophy, and that ethics should be formulated such that even the layman could meet its ends. After him lived Posidonius "the Athlete," born in Apamea in northern Syria around 135 B.C.E. He continued Posidonius' school in Rhodes where he taught both Greek and Roman scholars. He worked on philosophy, science, and history in his lifetime, but he held the Aristotelian view that philosophy was the master of the other two, directing their aims and ambitions and grounding their conclusions. He is responsible for the metaphor of the topoi or Stoic disciplines, calling physics the meat and blood, logic the bones and tendons, and ethics the soul.

The late Stoics get their start about 100 years after the middle Stoic period. Stoicism found a new home in the Roman Empire, its most famous proponents being Epictetus, Seneca, Cicero, and

Marcus Aurelius. Athens sent a delegation of the three major schools—the Academics, the Stoics and the Peripatetics—to Rome around 155 B.C.E. The initial envoy was unsuccessful, earning a backlash from the ruling class in Rome. 70 years later, in around 86 B.C.E., Greek philosophy finally found a home in the Empire with the establishment of Stoic and Epicurean schools.

Epictetus was born around 55 C.E. at Hierapolis, Phrygia. His name means "gained" or "acquired," signifying his birth as a slave. He was allowed by his master to study philosophy with Musonius Rufus, and influential Stoic sage, which bolstered his mind and his reputation. Around 68 C.E. he gained his freedom and began his life teaching philosophy in Rome. When in around 93 C.E. Emperor Domitian banished the philosophers, Epictetus moved to Nicopolis in Greece and there founded his school.

Epictetus believed that self-knowledge is at the center of philosophy, and, following Socrates, that the first aim of philosophical discourse is self-examination. To quote him directly on the matter, from book one, chapter fifteen of his *Discourses*,

"When a man was consulting him how he should persuade his brother to cease being angry with him, Epictetus replied: Philosophy does not propose to secure for a man any external thing. If it did philosophy would be allowing something which is not within its province. For as the carpenter's material is wood, and that of the statuary is copper, so the matter of the art of living is each man's life. "What then is my brother's?" That again belongs to his own art; but with respect to yours, it is one of the external things, like a piece of land, like health, like reputation. But Philosophy promises none of these. "In every circumstance, I will maintain," she says, "the governing part conformable to nature." Whose governing part? "His in whom I am," she says."[3]

Good alone, he says, is desirable, in opposition to rival schools that in one way or another emphasized pleasure's place in a fulfilled life. It is philosophy's job to provide the standard for good and evil, a task in its ability because both the mind and its products are, he says, of everything in creation, the only things entirely within our influence. When aware of the difference between these poles, an awareness that is based both on knowledge and habit, the wise person will be subject to the rightful order of the world.

What we have of Epictetus' works are not his own writings but lectures and discussions recorded by his student Arrian. Arrian says that Epictetus was the kind of speaker who could cause people to feel what he wanted them to feel when he wanted them to feel it. Arrian says that Epictetus lived a simple life, owning very few things, and though he never married, he

---

[3] Epictetus, *Discourses*, book one, chapter nine

adopted the child of a friend in his old age. He died around 135 C.E. of natural causes, having been admired in life by all who knew him.

Seneca was born around the turn of the 1st century C.E. in Cordoba, modern-day Spain. He became a citizen of Rome around 5 C.E., carried there by his mother's stepsister. Much of his early life is obscure to us, the evidence for it being scant. What we do know about him is primarily from after his rise to prominence within the Empire. Between C.E. 54 to C.E. 62, he acted as adviser to Nero. On the strength of his abilities in that position, he was also appointed consul in 56 C.E., an important political position in the Empire. Seneca is said to have played an important role in Boudica's rebellion in the recently conquered British territories by forcing loans onto the indigenous aristocracy before calling them in swiftly and with force. This episode may have contributed to the end of his political career.

Seneca wrote both philosophy and plays in his lifetime, in addition to his political writing. Much of his philosophical writing focuses on death and suffering and what one should do to defend oneself against grief and despair. His philosophy was decidedly Stoic, though he did have some eclectic influences, including Plato and the Aristotelians. Seneca wrote tragedies principally, including famous works like Agamemnon, Thyestes and Oedipus. The theme of many of his plays was revenge, a theme adopted by later playwrights influenced by Seneca like Shakespeare, Corneille, and Racine.

In 65 C.E. Seneca was ordered to kill himself by Emperor Nero on suspicion that he plotted to have the Emperor killed. Following tradition, he severed several of his veins in order to bleed to death. It is both unclear and unlikely that he had any involvement in the plot. Nonetheless, his death was slow and painful, owing to his advanced age and purportedly poor diet. In his will, he ordered that his body be cremated without funeral rites.

Cicero was born in 106 B.C.E. in Arpinium, south of Rome. His father was of the equestrian order, a propertied class below senators in Roman society, and thereby possessed a number of privileges and connections beyond the common citizen. From an early age, he learned both Latin and Greek by studying philosophers, rhetoricians, historians, and poets. Cicero used his bilingual tongue to translate and preserve many Greek texts, a proclivity in part responsible for his overwhelming influence during the Renaissance and the enlightenment.

Cicero is purported to have been a bright student who garnered attention from all corners of Roman society. It was little surprise, then, when he pursued a career in politics. He served both Gnaeus Pompeius Strabo and Lucius Cornelius Sulla in their campaigns in the Social War. Later, around 83 B.C.E., he began a career in law. His first major victory is recorded in 80 B.C.E. when he defended Sextus Roscius from the charge of patricide, a particularly serious case and a thorny matter in Roman society. In its aftermath, potentially to avoid the wrath of the dictator Sulla, whose allies Cicero had proven responsible for the murder of Roscius' father, Cicero traveled to Greece and Anatolia. In Athens, he studied with Antiochus of Ascalon, the founder of Middle Platonism, and in Anatolia he studied with leading rhetoricians, perfecting his skills as an orator.

In the conflict between Julius Caesar and Pompey, Cicero favored Pompey as the defender of Rome's Republican tradition. He was then forced to flee Rome when Caesar invaded Italy. He traveled with Pompey's forces for a time, at the same time losing faith in the Pompeian side. When Caesar won the civil war, Cicero returned to Rome and was pardoned. He did not participate in Caesar's assassination but was sympathetic to the cause. Mark Antony during the Second Triumvirate, however, in seeking revenge for Caesar's death, ordered Cicero killed because of his popularity and reputation. Cicero is reported to have, upon his capture, said: "There is nothing proper about what you are doing, soldier, but do try to kill me properly."

Marcus Aurelius was born the great-grandson of a praetor, the grandson of a patrician, reared in an extraordinarily wealthy family that had produced Emperors in the past. His father having died early, Marcus was raised by his grandfather, who taught him good character and the avoidance of bad temper. Marcus was taught at home by a number of tutors, including a leading Homeric scholar. After a hemorrhage, then Emperor Hadrian adopted Marcus' father-in-law with the intention that Marcus should rise to the throne. Even upon his appointment to serve under Antoninus, the consul for the year 139 C.E. and successor to Hadrian following the death of Marcus' father-in-law, Marcus is said to have acted with the same thrift and solemnity in his public role as when he was a private citizen.

As an Emperor, Marcus exercised and exemplified the Stoic virtues, earning the reputation as the last of the Five Good Emperors from Machiavelli. Marcus was proficient in imperial administration, versed in legislative theory. He commanded the Roman legions in several wars in his lifetime, with the Germanic tribes, with Parthia, and against the Marcomanni and the Sarmatians. During his campaigns he wrote his Meditations, a masterwork of philosophy still read widely by politicians and generals because of its wisdom in both political and military affairs, as well as its applicability to daily life.

Marcus Aurelius died in Vindobona, modern-day Vienna, on March 17th 180. Despite his orders, his ashes were returned to Rome, to Hadrian's mausoleum. There a column was built to commemorate his victories against the Germans and Sarmatians. His son Commodus succeeded him to the throne, despite the latter's unpredictable behavior and poor training in both politics and the military. It was nonetheless necessary that Commodus come to the throne to preserve peace in the Empire, to prevent another of the many succession wars in Roman history from tearing the Empire asunder.

The Roman Stoics emphasized therapeutic and theoretical aims over ethical and political activity, but almost all of the notable Roman figures were involved in politics in some capacity. Cato the Younger served as military tribune, praetor, and was a powerful opponent of Julius Caesar. Cicero, serving as a Roman Consul, taught himself Stoic ideas as one of the many schools he studied in his eclectic approach to philosophy. Athenodorus and Arius were counselors to Augustus Caesar. Seneca advised Nero. And Marcus Aurelius, of course, was Caesar of Rome. Covering each of these thinkers in detail is a task beyond the scope of this book; they each deserve their own book, chronicling their thoughts and deeds. I will nonetheless draw from several of them in this work.

This brief account of their history has shown that the Stoic school is diverse and malleable and has lived in many vastly different circumstances through its iterations. How are they all united? What allows them to keep the same name, despite the diversity in doctrine within the school? All Stoics accept the three topoi, ethics, logic, and physics. Their all teach virtue with the aim of living in accordance with human nature. Their logical systems include both the modern, formal definition, the study of what consequences follow from what premises, and epistemic concerns, concerns about the nature of knowledge and what human beings can know. Stoic physics includes the modern sense of the word, encompassing a variety of natural sciences, and metaphysics and theology. For the Stoics, the gods and the soul were physical beings, and studying them revealed their governing principles. This book will teach the nuts and bolts of all aspects of the *topoi* and will serve as a general introduction to Stoic ideas and practice.

The Good Life

"What is good?" This question is at the center of ethics. Before an ethical system can be constructed, criteria need to be established. For the ancients, and for many modern ethicists as well, the distinction between good and bad depend on life's aim. Those choices which approach or are in accord with life's aim are good. Those choices which frustrate or miss life's aim are bad. I mentioned in the introduction that the aim of the Stoic life is agreement with nature. That lifestyle and those actions that agree with fully developed human nature are virtuous, and those that do not are vicious. In this chapter, we will explore what "living in agreement or accord with nature" means in detail, virtue, and vice in general, and good and evil in particular. The goal is to ground your perceptions and your character in an unshakable foundation. As Epictetus says in book three, chapter six of his Discourses:

"The good man is invincible, for he does not enter the contest where he is not stronger. If you want to have his land and all that is on it, take the land; take his slaves, take his magisterial office, take his poor body. But you will not make his desire fail in that which it seeks, nor his aversion fall into that which he would avoid. The only contest into which he enters is that about things which are within the power of his will; how then will he not be invincible?"[4]

The Stoics think that, fundamentally, what is good exists in two places. First, a person may be good if they are well developed — if they are virtuous in character. Second, a person's choices may be good if, by choosing, he or she is exercising virtue. In the case of inner virtue, a person must develop a stable or durable disposition, such that their character endures life's tempests. In choice, a person must make a habit of virtuous activity, and this activity must be motivated by their virtuous character. If for example, one acts courageously because they do not know the danger of their situation, they are not for that reason good. If one is aware of the danger, that they may even be killed for pursuing a certain course but are directed by wisdom to uphold their duty, then their action is good.

There is a derivative sense of virtue in Stoicism which concerns objects. Whether or not choosing some sought after thing is virtuous is determined by generalization. Is it true that choosing the desired object is in all cases beneficial? In other words, does it always help people develop as human beings? This is not the case for money and power, for example. In the case of money, stories abound of spoiled children, corrupt businesses, and celebrity debauchery. Power gives those who would otherwise

---

[4]   Epictetus, *Discourses,* book three, chapter six

not act in untoward ways, though their character may be poor, license to practice their evil inclinations. We can extend these examples to a number of other possessions and trappings. Celebrity for its own sake gives the undisciplined spirit license to practice vanity. And security without fortitude, inner security against vice, invites sloth and indolence. Pleasure also does not meet this criterion. Against the Epicureans, for whom pleasure was life's aim, the Stoics argue that there are many pleasures that do not cultivate the individual. Knowledge, for example, considered a mental pleasure by Epicurus, may excite anger in an individual and thereby undermine their decision making. And in cases where pleasures do not make a person worse, they still may not make that person better. A choice of objects of this kind may be indifferent, but it is not virtuous. We should remember Epictetus' words when considering the difference between what is good and what is indifferent, and take to heart the reason for this distinction. In Chapter eight, book three of his *Discourses* he says,

"As we exercise ourselves against sophistical questions, so we ought to exercise ourselves daily against appearances; for these appearances also propose questions to us. "A certain person son is dead." Answer: the thing is not within the power of the will: it is not an evil. "A father has disinherited a certain son. What do you think of it?" It is a thing beyond the power of the will, not an evil. "Caesar has condemned a person." It is a thing beyond the power of the will, not an evil. "The man is afflicted at this." Affliction is a thing which depends on the will: it is an evil. He has borne the condemnation bravely." That is a thing within the power of the will: it is a good. If we train ourselves in this manner, we shall make progress; for we shall never assent to anything of which there is not an appearance capable of being comprehended."[5]

This discussion allows us to clarify a distinction not always made, between good and evil, virtue and vice, and positive and negative. For the Stoics, only choices can be good or evil. For example, in the previous paragraph, we looked at money, power, and pleasure and considered the value of pursuing them. But it is not money, power, or pleasure themselves that are good or indifferent, but our relationship to them. As Marcus Aurelius says in book six of his Meditations,

"The substance of the universe is obedient and compliant; and the reason which governs it has in itself no cause for doing evil, for it has no malice, nor does it do evil to anything, nor is anything harmed by it. But all things are made and perfected according to this reason."[6]

---

5 Epictetus, *Discourses,* book three, chapter eight
6 Marcus Aurelius, *Meditations,* book five

If we choose money over virtue, our choice is a bad one. Similarly, Stoics call another person's actions good or evil based on the choice involved.

When not a particular decision by a particular human being, choices are either virtuous or vicious. Those choices which are consistent with nature, that are good for any person, are virtuous. Choices such as these are directed by a well-developed faculty of choice and thereby called prudent or wise. Those choices that are inconsistent with human nature, that in some way degrade our character, are vicious. Choices such as these are made hastily and out of ignorance, thus they earn the name folly. Returning to the money example, if I cheat someone out of their life savings, I act evilly. But if I consider the choice of cheating someone out of their money abstractly, I judge that kind of action to be vicious. We will discuss virtue and vice further in the chapter dedicated to them.

Money, power, and pleasure outside the context of either concrete or abstract choices are externals. Externals can be positive, neutral, or negative. Positive externals are in some way fitting to our nature as human beings. Money, power, and pleasure may be positive externals in the right circumstances, for example, if the acquisition of money allows you to exercise prudence. They may also be neutral. Even of other people, Marcus Aurelius says in book five of the *Meditations*,

"In one respect man is the nearest thing to me, so far as I must do good to men and endure them. But so far as some men make themselves obstacles to my proper acts, man becomes to me one of the things which are indifferent, no less than the sun or wind or a wild beast. Now it is true that these may impede my action, but they are no impediments to my effects and disposition, which have the power of acting conditionally and changing."[7]

Negative externals are inconsistent with the nature of rational beings. The particular bad choices of others, while evil from the perspective of choice, are also negative from the perspective of externals. Money, power, and pleasure may also be negative under the right circumstances. If your money would allow you to act in a vicious way, it is a negative external. We will discuss externals at length in the chapter on what is and is not in our power.

To round off our discussion of good and bad, let us now look at the place of true and false judgments in determining value. The Stoics think that correct judgments about choices and externals affect how we feel. A well-developed character and faculty of choice knows the difference between virtue and vice in choice and positive and negative in externals. Further, the development of one's judgment is itself an object of morality. If I am not well developed, if I consistently choose externals over virtue, or

---

[7] *ibid*

choose externals that harm my character, I have bad judgment. Correct and incorrect judgments are products of my understanding of physics and logic. This is why the Stoics think physics and logic, the other two *to poi*, are necessary for a life in accordance with nature.

Correct judgments about choices also require that one knows what is in their power and what is not. Desiring what is not in one's power is not only contrary to nature, it is also a strain on human flourishing and an obstacle to a happy life. It is necessary, therefore, for you to learn what is and is not in your power if you are to transform Stoic moral theory into practical morality.

ON CONTROL

Fresh out of college, I had a lot on my plate. There were too many bills to count, too many job applications to apply for, and too many family members to satisfy. In six months I would have to begin loan repayments, and the local servicer was not shy in reminding me of the interest accumulating. Despite coming through the meat-grinder of higher education unscathed, I was more stressed than I'd ever been in college, with the exception of a few, dreadful finals weeks.

My solution was to bury my head in the sand. Though I applied for positions, and eventually landed one, I also avoided opening those friendly reminder letters, skirted several bill payments, and ran from the topic of my future goals. I managed in that period, but I did not live well. The best part of my day was the hours spent on the couch watching television after work, and only because I could avoid thinking about the cold steel in my chest every time an unknown number appeared on my caller id. In truth, I was miserable.

The deeper the ditch, the more rainwater it holds. My gradual, but consistent, retreat from responsibility left me bathed in rainwater without an umbrella. It was quick, but when the storm came, it was relentless. I'm embarrassed to say that I went without a phone for a while, I was trapped making large repayments, and I had been isolated from my family when I needed them most. And perhaps the worst part of it was that it was avoidable. I could have renegotiated my loans, I could have kept in touch with my family, and I could have budgeted my savings, but I didn't. I had goofed.

In his Enchiridion, the Roman Stoic Epictetus compares life to a play. No matter the circumstances we find ourselves in, he says, we must give the best performance we can. It would have been nice if I were born rich. Because most of my problems were money related, it would have saved me from drowning in my mess. But I also could have saved myself. Though the part handed to me wasn't ideal, I had messed up the performance. Specifically, I had not, under the weight of my burdens, shown resilience; I broke.

I failed in this instance because I did not recognize what was and what was not in my power. Marcus Aurelius says in book five of his *Meditations*,

"Things themselves touch not the soul, not in the least degree; nor have they admission to the soul, nor can they turn or move the soul: but the soul turns and moves itself alone, and whatever judgments it may think proper to make, such it makes for itself the things which present themselves to it."[8]

What is and is not in our power is a central Stoic theme and the heart of their ethics. To put it another way, the Stoics call us to

---

8   Marcus Aurelius, *Meditations*, book five

recognize what we control and what we do not. It was in my power to do all of the above, though they may not have turned out well anyway. It was also in my power to regulate my reaction to misfortune. Even of those problems that were unavoidable, I had the power to steel myself by recognizing that their outcomes didn't belong to me, by recognizing that they were externals.

Why is this distinction important? Epictetus says that if we are invested in what we do not control, then we invite unhappiness. This, he thinks, is akin to slavery because our well being is at the mercy of either other people or fate. If we leave ourselves open to external influences, it is as though we are inviting strangers into our home and expecting them to care for it when we do not even care for it ourselves.

There are three classes of things which Epictetus thinks are in our control. Opinions and judgments are the first. We are capable of changing our opinions when they are ill-formed and reassessing our judgments when they are incorrect. Choices and actions are the second. Both the development of our faculty of choice, our prohairesis, and our concrete decisions are at the core of who we are as individuals. Desires and aversions are the third. What we do, what we choose, influences our desires, as do our experiences. But if a desire is harmful, we can choose to avoid it, to wean ourselves off it, or to seek help in doing so.

Nothing else is in our control. Epictetus discusses poverty, disease, and death, for example. In part, these things are in our control. If I exercise and eat well, I can perhaps stave off disease and delay death. And if I do no work at all, poverty is almost guaranteed. But I cannot avoid death altogether—doing so is beyond my power. Similarly, I can take the greatest care in my hygiene and my health and still become sick, even fatally ill, from genetic diseases, cancer, or an inopportune handshake.

One pitfall Epictetus identifies lies in identifying oneself with one's possessions. We might recognize this today in various brand wars. Pepsi versus Coke, Apple versus Microsoft, GM or Ford versus a foreign car manufacturer—there are many tribes along brand lines. But we do not control the integrity of these brands or the quality of their products, unless, perhaps, you are an executive at one of these companies. Similarly, one might be complimented on their home, their clothes, or their cellphone. Even the love of knowledge and books can leave us vulnerable. Epictetus draws attention to this in book four chapter four of his *Discourses* when he says,

"Remember that not only the desire of power and of riches makes us mean and subject to others, but even the desire of tranquility, and of leisure. and of traveling abroad, and of learning. For, to speak plainly, whatever the external thing may be, the value which we set upon it places us in subjection to others. What, then, is the difference between desiring, to be a senator or not desiring to be one; what is the difference between desiring power or being content with a private station; what is the difference between saying, "I am unhappy, I have nothing, to do, but I am bound to my books as a corpse"; or saying, "I am unhappy, I have no leisure for reading"? For as salutations and power are things external and independent of the will, so is a book."[9]

But being complimented, or maligned, for these objects does not amount to a personal compliment or slight. You're not being called a good person because you have a nice cell phone. Epictetus gives a horse as an example. If a horse thinks of itself as handsome, it would make sense for a beautiful horse. But if you think that, because you have a beautiful horse, you're hot stuff, you're prideful of something that is not yours. That horse can be taken away; it belongs to you in title alone.

Epictetus thinks that we should limit what we consume. You may take pleasure in good food, fast cars, and nice clothes. I do, too. But if we indulge in these things, we open ourselves to desiring them. We give up some of our control to luxuries whose possession is not entirely our own. If we make ourselves vulnerable in this way, then we also make ourselves vulnerable to hurt if we lack them. In book three, chapter one of his Discourses Epictetus says:

---

[9]   Epictetus, *Discourses,* book four, chapter four

"'Thus, then, have we many masters?' We have: for we have circumstances as masters prior to our present masters; and these circumstances are many. Therefore it must of necessity be that those who have the power over any of these circumstances must be our masters. For no man fears Caesar himself, but he fears death, banishment, deprivation of his property, prison, and disgrace. Nor does any man love Caesar, unless Caesar is a person of great merit, but he loves wealth, the office of tribune, praetor or consul. When we love, and hate, and fear these things, it must be that those who have the power over them must be our masters. Therefore we adore them even as gods; for we think that what possesses the power of conferring the greatest advantage on us is divine."[10]

Unfortunately, most people leave themselves open to these desires and their accompanying pains. Whereas they should invest emotionally in only those things in their control, most people show slavish devotion to innumerable in differents. In doing so, they let those things in which they should take pride, their choices, desires, and opinions, atrophy.

Employing warfare as a metaphor, Epictetus says that we should not enter any battle we have not already won. By embracing those things that are in our control, we win the battle for happiness before it's waged. Those things in our control do not

---

[10] Epictetus, *Discourses*, book three, chapter one

admit opposition not of our own doing. Those things not in our control can require we vie with innumerable external factors, against none of which we are guaranteed of victory. And even if we to some degree obtain our desires, we may be yet unhappy. Epictetus thinks that even few external goods are enough for the person who wants nothing not in his control. But those who desire a lot, who want wealth, fame, and fortune, are too often never satisfied. Though they win battles, their campaigns do not succeed.

In his Discourses, Epictetus describes what we gain from proper attention to those things in and those things beyond our power. He describes the state that emerges from being attached only to what is in your power as tranquility. Progress toward tranquility is measured by the extent to which you're withdrawn from externals. You turn to your own will, to your own faculties, to that part of you which is most you. And in doing so, you exercise this innermost part. By labor, you improve it so that it conforms to human nature. This is the path to freedom. With it comes faithfulness and modesty. Epictetus says that if someone gave you away as a slave, you would be rightfully angry. Giving yourself away is what you do with your mind when you tie your well being to external things.

But what about those things that are assigned to us, though not belonging to us in the sense of being affected by our disposition or our will? For example, to what extent should I care for my son? If he does not take a bath, is failing in school, or is acting in untoward ways, to what extent am I responsible for his actions, and how do I differentiate that responsibility from those things that are or are not in my power? The Stoics here recognize duties. There are situations whose outcomes are not in my control, but there is an extent to which I am responsible, to which I can act, such that abrogation of that responsibility is an injury to myself. In the case of my son, though I cannot defeat fortune in the outcomes of my parenting, I can influence it by my action or inaction.

Similarly, I may have duties to my community. Like the temperament of our children, our parents, and sometimes even our friends and spouses, I cannot control the environment into which I am born. But I do not have to be impassive. Epictetus says in his Enchiridion,

"Duties are universally measured by relations. Is anyone a father? If so, it is implied that the children should take care of him, submit to him in everything, patiently listen to his reproaches, his correction. But he is a bad father. Are you naturally entitled, then, to a good father? No, only to a father. Is a brother unjust? Well, keep your own situation towards him. Consider not what he does, but what you are to do to keep your own faculty of choice in a state conformable to nature."

We saw in the brief historical sketch that it was not uncommon for the Stoics, particularly the later Stoics, to be involved in politics. How do we square this with the doctrine of control? It helps to think about our political responsibilities in relation to our concentric circles of care or concern. The innermost circle, consisting of our immediate family, is considered by the Stoics the most important. As the circle expands, to friends, to neighbors, to countrymen, and to the whole of humanity, our concern becomes more distant, our attachment more remote. Developing our concern to the limits of the circle is, for the Stoics, a kind of development of our sense of justice. It is not difficult to treat our family and our friends in a way becoming of their circumstances, that fulfills what they are owed. It is far more difficult, and a test that we live by principle, to treat strangers with equanimity. On this point, remember the words of Emperor Marcus Aurelius from book three of his Meditations:

"For the lot which is assigned to each man is carried along with him and carries him along with it. And he remembers also that every rational animal is his kinsman, and that to care for all men is according to man's nature, and a man should hold on to the opinion not of all, but of those only who confessedly live according to nature."[11]

---

11   Marcus Aurelius, *Meditations*, book three

Virtue in Stoicism

The Stoics think that virtue, moral goodness, is not just sufficient for happiness, it's necessary. In his Stoic Paradoxes, Cicero says that if you value something other than virtue, you will eventually be unhappy. What happiness you may derive from externals is not genuine, both because it is founded upon the mere appearance of what is good for you, and because it is flimsy, fleeting. Happiness built upon externals is subject to fortune, while that happiness which comes from virtue is self-sufficient.

Understanding virtue is both a cognitive and a practical state of being. One must know the character of the virtues, their description, and the distinction between them in order to practice them. But likewise one must know them in practice, through habit and application, to fully grasp their meaning. Cicero says that if we have an interwoven conceptual and experiential map of the virtues, we will also understand why happiness is impossible without them.

Zeno says that each virtue is a kind of wisdom. What exactly he meant by this sparked a debate between his successors, Cleanthes and Chrysippus. Cleanthes thought that all the virtues were wisdom. To put it another way, he thought that in every circumstance where we exercise, prudence, courage, temperance, etc, what we are really exercising is wisdom in different circumstances. Chrysippus thought that each virtue was a type or branch of wisdom. For him, the virtues really were distinct, and they receive the name "virtues" because wisdom is their common property.

Their meaning might become apparent if we consider them carefully. First Cleanthes. If all the virtues are one in the way he means, what is, for example, courage? Courage would be in part a kind of knowledge about what is and is not to be feared and how we should behave in the face of that which threatens us. The other half of courage would be knowledge about the exercise of this first knowledge; a kind of second-order knowledge. But what can we say about the difference between this knowledge and, say, prudence or practical wisdom? They would both be a kind of knowledge, and the object of both kinds, in the second-order version, is a correct exercise of that knowledge. But is everything which we call prudence also courage? What of returning to my friend something he has loaned? Should we say that there is no difference between the correct choice in circumstances like this and those in which my life or my well-being is in danger? I might need new friends if the prospect of returning what is owed to them is a source of disturbance!

What, then, if we do consider the virtues as separate as Chrysippus would, but as all branches or kinds of wisdom instead of all being the same wisdom but in different circumstances? This view seems to more accurately describe the relationship between the virtues as an interconnected we. Under this view, we can explain why, for example, prudence without justice is not a virtue: In the case, I might choose correctly how to carry out some or another aim, but that aim is something like murder or theft. I am therefore wise with respect to my execution, but unwise in what I desire to do. It is for the sake of examples like these, and in fidelity to the kinds of behavior we refer to in English when we use the words "wise" "prudent" and "just," that I will assume Chrysippus' explanation of the relationship between the virtues from here forward.

The Stoics hold that human nature has certain propensities (oikeiôsis) for moral development. Beyond being fully developed human nature, virtue is a state toward which we unconsciously, maybe even by instinct, tend. When we learn to reason during and after childhood, we can then refine our instincts through habituation.

The Stoics identify three drives belonging to every human. First, we act to achieve our goals and interests. These include wealth, security, health, etc. Second, we identify with the interests of others. We start with our immediate family, then our friends, fellow citizens, and finally humanity as a whole. Third, we reason about and solve the problems facing us in life. These drives or propensities require the virtues if they're to be successful. We need courage and temperance if we are to achieve our goals. To exercise our concern for the expanding circle of people, we require justice. And prudence or a well-developed faculty of choice empowers us to confront life's problems.

Along with the cardinal virtues, there are a number of specific virtues under each class. Temperance divides into honor, self-control, and propriety. Prudence breaks into good judgment (as arises from knowledge of logic and physics), discretion, and resourcefulness. Justice is comprised of kindness, piety, and sociability. And courage can be divided into perseverance, magnanimity, and confidence.

The cardinal virtues, considered as wisdom, show the kind of inseparability Zeno referred to. Prudence, wisdom applied to living in a society or with others generally in your circle of concern, is justice. Endurance in work and life and in the face of fears and hardships is wisdom in the form of courage. And wisdom in choice and aversion, and in emotional attachment, is temperance. One might even go so far as to say, as Chrysippus did, that the virtues form a kind of web. For example, if I do not show wisdom in my choices, I cannot choose to endure a difficult situation. And if I am not just, if I do not show wisdom in my relationships with others, I will be intemperate in my relationships, taking too much or too little without contributing in turn.

Cicero says that justice consists in giving others what they deserve. The end of justice is, first, treating others in a way that benefits both parties involved. This is akin to honoring a contract, one whose first clause is not to do harm. Beyond the advantage of both parties, however, justice also serves and advances the ends of human society as a whole. By fulfilling our duties with regard to justice we bolster trust in cooperation between all parties involved in agreements. Opposed to justice is injustice, which Cicero, in his *On Duties*, describes as follows:

"Now the foundation of justice is faithfulness, which is a perseverance and truth in all our declarations -and in all our promises. Let us therefore (though some people may think it over nice) imitate the Stoics, who curiously examine whence terms are derived, and consider that the word faithfulness (jides), is no other than a performance of what we have premised. But there are two kinds of injustice; the first is of those who offer an injury, the second of those who have it in their power to avert an injury from those to whom it is offered, and yet do it not."[12]

Courage is also called greatness of strength or of the noble spirit. This is not what we typically consider courage to be, but it is, for the Stoics, its defining characteristic. Not only does it involve attaining those things that make our lives better, whether

---

12   Cicero, *On Duties*

through hard work and discipline or through endurance, but also in rising above what we have acquired. Insofar as bettering ourselves in any way requires us to face difficulties and challenges and to rise above our present condition, it is an act of courage.

The latter aspect of rising above what we gain, orderly behavior and self-control, the Stoics call temperance. A certain amount of propriety in daily life conserves what is good tout court and what is befitting of any particular situation.

The virtues are also closely connected in structure with the three *topoi*, logic, ethics, and physics. The three *topoi* correspond to three Stoic disciplines—desire, action, and assent. Let's look briefly at each of these disciplines and how they tie the *topoi* to the virtues. Epictetus says of these three disciplines in his *Enchiridion*,

"The first and most necessary topic in philosophy is that of the use of moral theorems, such as, 'We ought not to lie;' the second is that of demonstrations, such as, 'What is the origin of our obligation not to lie'" the third gives strength and articulation to the other two, such as, "What is the origin of this is a demonstration.' For what is demonstration? What is consequence? What contradiction? What truth? What falsehood? The third topic, then, is necessary on the account of the second, and the second on the account of the first. But the most necessary, and that whereon we ought to rest, is the first. But we act just on the contrary. For we spend all our time on the third topic, and employ all our diligence about that, and entirely neglect the first. Therefore, at the same time that we lie, we are immediately prepared to show how it is demonstrated that lying is not right."[13]

Desire derives from physics. One must train to want only what is possible and to ignore what the universe doesn't allow. For the Stoics, this well-maintained desire is rooted in cause and effect. Through acquaintance with what the causes of circumstances and events are, one is steeled against outcomes inconsistent with what is in one's own power. Of course, extreme examples involve the desire to live forever or to live a life without suffering. But also included are desires involving other people, for them to never disappoint you or to do what is contrary to their nature or moral development. Desire is therefore linked to courage and temperance. Courage, in this case, is endurance in the face of fortune, good and bad. Temperance, in this case, is well-regulated desire. The Stoics refer to desire as the doctrine of acceptance.

Action, also called Stoic philanthropy, is the idea that humans ought to develop concern for others that is in accord with the exercise of justice. This is the discipline closest ethics. The Stoics

---

13   Epictetus, *Enchiridion*

believe that we exist for other people, to teach them and to develop with them. If we can do neither, we should at least suffer their faults, aware that they are also reflections of our own follies.

Assent is also called Stoic mindfulness. We make choices about which experiences we accept and reject. Knowing what lessons are to be drawn is related to prudence. It is therefore dependent upon logic. Assent also governs opinion. If I believe something, I am giving assent to it. But if I believe things without sufficient evidence, I am imprudent with respect to my opinions. And perhaps the most important beliefs I have concern the nature of the cosmos as a whole and my place within it.

STOIC LOGIC AND YOU

We come now to a branch of Stoic philosophy not often discussed, and not discussed in great detail where it is mentioned: Stoic logic. Prudence, practical wisdom about matters great and small in ethical life, owes its power to both logic and physics, where the former studies what consequences follow from what premises and the latter supplies the premises for sound arguments. If we are to make prudent decisions, to judge when and to what extent specific actions are to be taken, we must have firm support upon which to ground and to justify our choices. Epictetus makes this point well in chapter seven, book one of his *Discourses* when he says,

"For what is the end proposed in reasoning? To establish true propositions, to remove the false, to withhold assent from those which are not plain. Is it enough then to have learned only this? "It is enough," a man may reply. Is it, then, also enough for a man, who would not make a mistake in the use of coined money, to have heard this precept, that he should receive the genuine drachmae and reject the spurious? "It is not enough." What, then, ought to be added to this precept? What else than the faculty which proves and distinguishes the genuine and the spurious drachmae? Consequently also in reasoning what has been said is not enough; but is it necessary that a man should acquire the faculty of examining and distinguishing the true and the false, and that which is not plain? "It is necessary."[14]

In this chapter, we will discuss Stoic logic in particular, but the Stoics do not exhaust the field. As always, I encourage you to seek other sources and to study other kinds of logic if you find the coming discussion interesting or helpful.

The reasons for modern disinterest in Stoic logic are many. The field has moved far beyond the concepts available to the ancients since the development of modern logic, due in large part to Gottlob Frege and Bertrand Russell. And many modern Stoics are more interested in ethical doctrines psychological insights than the nuts and bolts of ancient Stoic cannon—with good reason. But the greatest hurdle to any engagement with Stoic logic is the scarcity of surviving works. We know, as previously mentioned, that Chrysippus alone wrote dozens of texts exploring a range of logical topics, none of which survive. What remains is gathered from a number of disparate sources, some of which contain conflicting testimonies and unreliable accounts. In the interest of providing consistent exposition, I will draw primarily from two authors: Sextus Empiricus and Diogenes Laertius. Combined, I think, they chart a robust logical theory that I hope here to make both digestible and useful for the application of Stoic ethics.

---

14   See Epictetus, *Discourses,* book one, chapter seven

Our discussion of Stoic logic will begin with their theory of meaning or a semantic theory in modern parlance. For the Stoics, words mean what can be said in a particular language, and what can be said stands for objects in the world. To put it another way, what can be said are expressions of thoughts, and thoughts correspond to the objects about which they are thought. If I point to a particular plant and say "tree," the word signifies a thought in my head, the object of which is the observed plant. On an alternative view of meaning in Stoicism, what can be said does not correspond directly with what is thought, but derives meaning from other words which, as a complex web, are related indirectly to thought. Under this view, the sentence "that is a tree" gains its meaning from the grammatical use of the words in combination, and the combination of words has a fuzzy or imperfect relationship with the thoughts in our head. For our purposes, it is enough to assume the first theory and to not wade too deeply into this rich, but difficult, debate.

That quick detour accomplished, let us turn now to Stoic semantics. Stoic syllogisms, arguments consisting of two premises and one conclusion, are propositional, meaning that the terms involved are whole propositions. Contrast this to Aristotelian logic, often called predicate logic because its terms were subjects, that which is affirmed or denied, and predicates, that which is affirmed or denied of the subject. The most familiar Aristotelian syllogism is of the figure 1) All birds are animals. 2)

All crows are birds. 3) Therefore, all crows are animals. Arguments of this kind, in which the middle term connects two universal statements, are one type of syllogism identified by Aristotle. He called it the first figure. But Aristotle's syllogism, though powerful in its own right, cannot in any figure handle arguments with complex premises like 1) If my dog is barking, the mailman has arrived. 2) My dog is barking. 3) Therefore, the mailman has arrived. Stoic logic, however, can parse arguments with complex premises.

Stoic arguments may be classified in several ways, first into valid and invalid arguments. For the Stoics, an argument is valid when the conditional (if-then) has the conjunction of its premises as its antecedent and the conclusion as its consequence, and that consequence is evaluated "true." In the previous example of my dog and the mailman, the conjoined antecedents are premises 1 and 2 and the consequence is 3. If both of the antecedents are fulfilled, then the consequence must be true, therefore the argument is valid. You are likely familiar with a version of this definition of validity already, so I will not spend too much time with it here.

Next, a valid argument is either true or not true. In a true argument, both the premises and the conclusion are evaluated true. This is best shown by an example of a not true valid argument. 1) If my dog is barking, the sun will rise. 2) My dog is barking. 3) The sun will rise. The argument is valid because if the conjunction of the antecedents hold, the conclusion must follow. But premise 1 is clearly false; my dog's barking does not always mean the sun will rise. She may just as well bark in the middle of the night. Though the argument is valid, then, it is not true. This is also likely familiar to you already. Today we call this the distinction between a sound and an unsound argument.

True valid arguments may be demonstrative or not demonstrative. Demonstrative arguments show something new or not-evident from premises that are already recognized to be the case or that are evident. For an example of this kind of argument, I will turn to Sextus Empiricus' Outlines of Pyrrhonism. There he says "1) If sweat flows through the surface of the skin, there exist imperceptible pores. 2) Sweat flows through the surface of the skin. 3) Therefore, there exist imperceptible pores." These are the kinds of arguments we often see in the disciplines, whether they be in the sciences or the humanities. If an argument does not yield a novel conclusion, then it is not demonstrative. The Stoics also recognize undemonstrated arguments, which purport to yield new information but have not yet been proven. We might think of these as untested hypotheses, or as arguments in a greater chain of reasoning whose demonstration depends on the conclusion of that chain. They are not to be confused with not demonstrative arguments which yield no new information. At this point note that whether an argument is undemonstrated or demonstrated may vary with respect to time. This temporality is a curious feature of Stoic logic to which we will return later.

Demonstrated true valid arguments may proceed through memory and belief alone toward their conclusion or may proceed through memory and belief and discovery. I will again turn to Sextus Empiricus for an example of an argument whose conclusion is reached through memory and belief alone. Again in Outlines of Pyrrhonism, he says "1) If someone said to you that this man would be wealthy, this man will be wealthy. 2) This god said to you that this man would be wealthy. 3) Therefore, this man will be wealthy." Sextus says that assent to the conclusion of this argument depends on the belief in the god and in the god's assertion. There is an example closer in structure and assumption to our own time I think we can use. 1) If an official says the war would go well, the war will go well. 2) The president says the war would go well. 3) The war will go well. Assent to this argument depends not upon the necessity of its premises, but upon our trust in the current president. Of those demonstrated arguments requiring both memory or belief and discovery, Sextus' pore example is an instance. We require an assumption or belief that moisture does not flow through solid bodies.

Undemonstrated arguments have two forms, those which may be demonstrated in time as mentioned above and those which are non-temporal. Those undemonstrated arguments that are non-temporal are referred to as "inference schemata." There are five such non-temporal undemonstrated arguments into whose forms all other true and valid arguments in Stoic logic fall. We will take a brief look at each of them now and then move on to applications of Stoic logic in Stoic ethics.

The first non-temporal undemonstrated is today known as modus ponendo ponens. It is the form of argument we have, to this point, been using in our examples. If p, then q; p; therefore, q. As we've seen, this schemata has a conditional and its antecedent as premises, followed by the consequent of the conditional as its conclusion. As Epictetus says in book two, chapter six of his *Discourses*,

"The hypothetical proposition is indifferent: the judgment about it is not indifferent, but it is either knowledge or opinion or error. Thus life is indifferent: the use is not indifferent. When any man then tells you that these things also are indifferent, do not become negligent; and when a man invites you to be careful, do not become abject and struck with admiration of material things. And it is good for you to know your own preparation and power, that in those matters where you have not been prepared, you may keep quiet, and not be vexed if others have the advantage over you. For you, too, in syllogisms will claim to have the advantage over them; and if others should be vexed at this, you will console them by saying, "I have learned them, and you have not." Thus also where there is need of any practice, seek not that which is required for the need, but yield in that matter to those who have had practice, and be yourself content with firmness of mind."[15]

The second schemata is today known as modus tollendo tollens. Its form is as follows: If p, then q; not q; therefore, not-p. For this schemata, the conditional and the contradiction of its consequence as premises. From that, the contradiction of the antecedent follows as the conclusion. I will provide a brief example. 1) If I am going to the car wash, then my car will be cleaned. 2) My car will not be cleaned (or not-my car will be cleaned. 2) Therefore, I am not going to the car wash (or not-I am going to the car wash).

The third schemata is nameless, but it should nonetheless be familiar. Its form is: Not p and q; p; therefore, not-q. We may phrase this as "not both" p and q. So, for example, 1) Not both x is good and x is evil. 2) x is good. 3) Therefore, not x is evil. In this schemata a negative conjunction is the premise along with one of its conjuncts (so p and q, and p respectively in this case). The necessary conclusion, then, is the contradiction of the remaining conjunct.

Schemata four is today called modus ponendo tollens. Its form is as follows: Either p or q; p; therefore, not-q. For example, 1) Either I will go to college or I will work in my parents' bakery. 2)

---

[15] Epictetus, *Discourses*, book two, chapter six

I will work in my parents' bakery. 3) Therefore, I will not go to college (or not-I will go to college). In this schemata a disjunction and one of its disjuncts are premises. The conclusion then is the contradiction of the remaining disjunct.

Finally, schemata five is today known as modus tollendo ponens. Either p or q; not-q; therefore, p. For example, 1) Either I will go to college or I will work in my parents' bakery. 2) I will not work in my parents' bakery (or not-I will work in my parents' bakery). 3) Therefore, I will go to college. In this schemata the disjunct and the contradiction of one of its disjuncts are premises. It follows, then, that the other disjunct is the conclusion.

Logic as an aid to Stoic teachings serve our inner life, that we do not live in a cloud of confusion in matters of right and wrong, and that we do not thereby choose vice instead of virtue. Epictetus gives a number of examples and deploys metaphor in describing the importance of sound arguments. We can explore more contemporary examples. If a friend tells me that my time with them is too short, that I am abusive because of my inattention, and thereby concludes that I am either actively malicious or at least indifferent to their feelings, might we consider this an argument of the fourth or the fifth schemata? If the fifth, my friend is saying that I am either indifferent or malicious. If I deny my intentions are malicious, they will call me indifferent instead, justifying their ire. If I want to avoid this trap, I should deny their original disjunction as false by asserting a third option into their dilemma.

That example was simple enough, what about a more difficult one? Say I am dealing with a difficult colleague. After requesting she complete a task for me, she tells me that she will be away for the weekend. Do I lose my temper with her? In the case that I do, my reasoning could be something like this: I can't both keep a level head and avoid being trampled on and disrespected by her. Superficially this choice seems to match the form of schema three; not-I can keep a level head and keep my dignity. But we can reveal the deceptiveness of this dilemma via the first two schemata. For example, the inference "if I do not lose my temper, then I will be disrespected" can be proven false by considering whether or not it has been demonstrated in the past. Is it true that in all cases where I do not lose my temper I am disrespected, or is there another way I can express myself? Similarly, the implication "If I lose my temper, I will be respected" can be reflected on. Does a short fuse lead to respect in every circumstance? Does it lead to respect in any circumstance? The Stoics would say no, but I leave it to you to decide. When you do so, remember the difference between respect and intimidation.

There are a number of other examples I could introduce, but lived experience and active reflection are, I think, the best ways to learn Stoic rules of inference and Stoic logic. We are not quite done with these rules; we will see them again in all the following chapters indirectly, and in more explicit form when discussing some of the logical pitfalls identified by cognitive behavioral therapy and more immediately in thinking about Stoicism in its relationship with theology.

Cosmology and Theology in Stoicism

Stoic ethics is incomplete without a discussion of the Divine Fire. In ethics, philosophers concern themselves with what it means to be moral, what moral living consists of, and the status of moral knowledge. But no less important to them is the question "why be moral?" Living a morally upright life, being a "moral saint" as contemporary philosopher Susan Wolf describes it, is often more difficult than living a viscous, immoral life. Part of the Stoic answer to this question is that virtue is human nature. Under this account, it is for our own benefit that we pursue virtue, so that we can achieve those ends which nature has given us, whether socially, psychologically, or spiritually. But this is only half of the Stoic response to the "why be moral?" question. Reason two is that the life in accordance with nature brings us into harmony with the will of the cosmos, the Divine Fire. As Epictetus says in his *Enchiridion*,

"Be assured that the essential property of piety towards the gods is to form right opinions concerning them, as existing "I and as governing the universe with goodness and justice. And fix yourself in this resolution, to obey them, and yield to them, and willingly follow them in all events, as produced by a perfect understanding. For thus you will never find fault with the gods, nor accuse them of neglecting you."[16]

The extent to which Divine Fire is essential to Stoicism is a matter for debate among modern Stoics. I will not wade waist deep into that argument. Divine Fire is, at its heart, a pantheist idea. It portrays the entire universe, the all, as in some way infused with divinity. But I don't think it is foreign to us in the west in particular, and to many world religions in general. We might recognize parts of Stoic pantheism in Deism, in which reason and observation are sufficient to discover God's will. To the extent that Divine Fire rejects revealed religion, we can say it is incompatible with most strains of Christianity, Hinduism, Islam, and Judaism. But I do not, for that reason alone, think Divine Fire in any way threatens the major religions of our time. And, at any rate, I do not think it is necessary to assent to or deny this Stoic doctrine to understand its place in Stoic ethics.

The "all" for the Stoics has the character of a sphere. This great copula encloses everything that is, and in it all forces, inward and outward, are balanced. Stoicism, taken as a whole, is meant to mirror this balance; it is meant to enclose and relate all aspects of conscious experience. To that extent, Stoicism includes both reason and logic and the natural sciences on the one hand, and faith on the other. These two sides—I'll call them reason and

---

16   Epictetus, *Enchiridion*

faith for brevity, though I don't mean to imply that they are really opposed—are united by and in cosmology for the Stoics. In Stoic cosmology, the universe was born from and is driven by Divine Fire.

There are two sides to Divine Fire, the passive and active principles. The passive principle is matter without purpose. We might think of this as non-living objects, though they are, at best, the outward manifestations of this principle. Taken generally, it is that in the universe which is acted upon but does not itself act. The active principle may be thought of as the organizing principle or the law of attraction. It is what causes the passive principle to manifest as all those things in the universe which we recognize. We might also refer to the active principle as the consciousness of the universe. We, of course, recognize the outward form of this consciousness in living creatures. The Stoics say that we, as with all living creatures, are sparks of this second aspect of Divine Fire. As Marcus Aurelius says in book four of his *Meditations*,

"Constantly regard the universe as one living being, having one substance and one soul; and observe how all things have reference to one perception, the perception of this one living being; and how all things act with one movement; and how all things are the cooperating causes of all things which exist;

observe too the continuous spinning of the thread and the texture of the web."[17]

Living in accordance with nature is the aim of Stoic philosophy because by doing so we live out our existence as sparks of divinity. If we do not follow this maxim, we not only harm ourselves, we harm the whole of existence. If we follow only our own interests, we introduce disharmony. Divine Fire, then, is a kind of Divine Command Theory—we follow the moral law because the Divine commands it. Further, what benefits the whole also benefits us. This idea, that we serve the whole first and thereby serve ourselves turns the idea that by following the moral law we serve ourselves on its head. Whereas the latter is a kind of egoism, says that ultimately self-development is what matters, the doctrine of Divine Fire says that ultimately the whole is what matters, and serving our own interests is a pleasant side effect. We are passive insofar as we follow this maxim, but active insofar as we, possessed of the divine spark, decide the very universal maxim we follow. We must be prepared to and may be called to, sacrifice our own interests if thereby a greater, moral purpose is served.

This idea of self-sacrifice as fallen into disrepute in the 21st century, and for good reason. Both countries and religions have called on individuals to give up their particular interests for a

---

17   Marcus Aurelius, *Meditations*, book four

universal value, whether it be nation or dogma. But we should divorce these (I think incorrect) calls for self-effacement from the kind of sacrifice championed in religion, meaningful political activity, and in Stoic doctrine. Whereas the former reduces the individual to parts of a greater project, the latter situate the project firmly in the individuals themselves. In Christianity, Christ lives in His subjects; in democracy, the free citizen is preserved in individual activity; in Stoicism, the Divine Fire expresses itself in moral agents. Sacrifice in extreme circumstances may involve suffering, but the foundation of that sacrifice is the conflict in each person between their particular interests and the projects they choose and enact. Rather than being irrelevant to the project, rather than being dispensable, we are first indispensable if the project is to be made manifest and second responsible for deciding what that project is. This is more in line with Stoic teachings than either nationalism or wars for religion.

Stoicism and Psychology

Cognitive Behavioral Therapy, or CBT for short, is an innovative approach to psychotherapy that has flourished in the last several decades. Through the NHS, the British government has dedicated hundreds of millions to training and equipping psychologists in and with its techniques. Its founders, Albert Ellis and Aaron Beck, drew heavily from the Stoic and Socratic traditions in developing a holistic therapy, the aim of which is self-evaluation. Through this approach, the analysand is encouraged to bring their unconscious beliefs to the forefront, to address and defeat those beliefs which contribute to their illness.

Its creators stripped CBT of ethics, values, and any mention of a higher purpose or meaning and gave the ancient teachings that inspired it a scientific basis. In doing so, however, they stripped away the center of these teachings, reducing them to, at best, empirically founded self-help guides. In opposition to this approach, new schools of CBT have arisen. They include Acceptance and Commitment Therapy, positive psychology, and mindfulness-CBT. They include questions of value in therapy, and thereby involve a more robust concept of the human subject in their tool-box approach to cognitive renewal.

In his book, The Philosophy of CBT, Donald Robertson traces the roots of this modern therapeutic practice back to the ancient Greeks and Romans. For him, drawing on the comportment of the ancients, philosophy, and therapy are not entirely distinct. Ancient philosophy studied the "art of living," changing the philosopher's attitudes to alter and improve their lives. This is different from the interests of psychotherapists, whose preoccupation is health, and specifically mental health. Nonetheless, philosophers and therapists can still learn much from each other. Philosophers can gain ideas for the practical application of philosophical study, and therapists can learn concepts, strategies, and techniques that are consistent with modern models of therapy, though largely neglected.

The aim of drawing out the link between CBT and philosophy is to clarify concept and value-based issues, to strengthen psychological changes made by the former and include the reflective approach of the latter. Philosophical counseling integrated into cognitive behavioral therapy employs concepts like human flourishing, resilience, and the good life, advocating both particular healing, addressing individual and long-term problems, and lifetime results and self-reliance, integrating its lessons into a schema or framework for living well.

CBT employs an onion model of the mind. Thoughts we have, positive or negative, are usually signs of underlying beliefs. If you experience social anxiety, for example, you might believe that other people are judgmental or don't like you, or that you yourself are unlikable. These thoughts, in turn, influence your behavior. You might shy away from others or going out entirely to avoid confirming your fears. This becomes a viscous cycle; negative thoughts and emotions are reinforced by your actions, which in turn influence your thoughts and emotions. CBT aims to disrupt this cycle by analysis. Similarly, Epictetus treats anxiety as related to the doctrine of control when in chapter 13, book two of his *Discourses* he says,

"When I see a man anxious, I say, "What does this man want? If he did not want something which is not in his power, how could he be anxious?" For this reason a lute player when he is singing by himself has no anxiety, but when he enters the theatre, he is anxious even if he has a good voice and plays well on the lute; for he not only wishes to sing well but also to obtain   applause: but this is not in his power. Accordingly, where he has a skill, there he has confidence. Bring any single person who knows nothing of music, and the musician does not care for him. But on the matter where a man knows nothing and has not been practiced, there he is anxious."[18]

Through behavioral experiments, you can change your thoughts and improve your lifestyle. You can take your fears head-on and reassess the beliefs which fuel them. At the same time, you learn about human psychology, and about the mechanisms by which negative thoughts are reinforced.

---

18   Epictetus, *Discourses,* book two, chapter thirteen

CBT aims to correct those errors in thinking which lead to emotional disturbances. The literature on the topic includes a list of the errors which typically lead to harmful, self-destructive thinking. The analysand is taught to be on guard for those automatic thoughts that create negative ideas and emotions. The aim is to, when in any kind of emotional distress, confront the disruptive, core beliefs that lie a layer deeper. Though I can't here exhaust the therapeutic methods employed by cognitive behavioral therapy, I will touch on some common errors pointed out in the literature. This attitude is present in the Stoics, too. For example, when Epictetus in his *Enchiridion* says,

"Does anyone bathe in a mighty little time? Don't say that he does it ill, but in a mighty little time. Does anyone drink a great quantity of wine? Don't say that he does ill, but that he drinks a great quantity. For, unless you perfectly understand the principle from which anyone acts, how should you know if he acts ill? Thus you will not run the hazard of assenting to any appearances but such as you fully comprehend."[19]

The principle of thinking through our disturbances exemplified here is at the hear of the CBT method of therapy.

One common error is the overgeneralization. The core of this error is a kind of hyperbole. When some negative event happens, or some perceived personality or behavioral defect appears, the

---

19 Epictetus, *Enchiridion*

person experiencing it tends to think that it happens all the time, or that the flaw is in some way essential to them as a person. If, for example, I'm in a situation where I make some social gaffe or slight someone unintentionally, I might deride myself as socially inept or antisocial. And if I fail to complete a task, or fail to complete one well, I might call myself incompetent or stupid, turning a temporary error into just another example of my ineptitude.

Another error is in the attribution of blame. In some cases, one might take any criticism or negative remark as a comment about their own worth. Alternately, in the same vein, accidents of fortune or mistakes others have made are personalized. If for example, someone tells me my presentation could use work or is below expectation, I am making a mistake if I tie my own worth to the success of a single project. Or if my computer stops working or some critical software has a bug or a virus, I might scold myself for not taking better care of it, or for not backing up my files when I had the chance. The other half of this error is taking too little blame or blaming others. If my truck stops working while an employee has it, it would be incorrect for me to blame the employee if it is my responsibility to change the battery, to ensure the vehicle is in good condition.

Black and white thinking is a third kind of error referred to in the literature. This is another way we might exaggerate a situation, good or bad. If I did poorly on an exam, for instance, I might say I have completely blown my chances for a good grade. On the other hand, if I do well, I might become lax, thinking I've overcome the greatest hurdle the class has to offer.

A common error in our thinking, related to over generalizing, is jumping to conclusions. Is there sufficient evidence for me to believe something about the future? If I, before going to a party, say to myself that I will be an embarrassment or a "drag" socially, am I really justified in saying that? Or, if someone else gives me a sly look or a look I find insulting, is it right for me to jump to the conclusion that they don't like me or that they are plotting against me? Often these mistakes occur because of bad experiences in the past. But are these experiences reason to think the present or the future holds the same pitfalls?

CBT also warns us against incorrectly moralizing a situation. Good and bad only apply to actions and choices, as we've seen in the chapter on Stoic morality. So if I, after experiencing some misfortune outside of my control, say that it should or ought to have gone another way, I am mistaken in externalizing a moral imperative. There is no particular way that an event outside of my control should or ought to have gone. Only my actions and my disposition toward fortune should be some way or another. Of those things over which I have no control, I can declare no obligation for them to produce one result or another.

The last error we'll look at is the error of mental filtering. This error involves selective sight of either positive or negative events. Alternatively, we might notice when something nice happens to us, but value it less than negative events. If someone compliments me for an accomplishment, I might dismiss them as just being nice, or even twist their complement into a slight. "You did well on this exam" can become "you haven't done well on the others," or "you did well, but I did better."

CBT uses a variety of techniques to address these and other errors. We start by pointing out the error, then we examine and criticize it. First, we ask ourselves what error applies to the negative thought or emotion we are experiencing. Then we look at the facts of the matter. Is there evidence for what we're feeling? Is there evidence against it? The facts become weights or reasons by which we can judge our thinking correct or incorrect.

After the thought has been examined in detail, the next step is to be both honest and sympathetic with ourselves. CBT calls us not to use double standards. Instead of being tough on ourselves, of talking down to ourselves about what errors we make, we should treat ourselves as we would a good friend. We don't hide the mistakes we make; the point of searching for the errors was, in the first place, in the service of honesty. But we also should not be flippant toward our negative emotions, nor should we seek to tear ourselves down over what may be honest mistakes in our thinking.

Next, we are warned against "all or nothing" thinking. Think, instead, of a continuum in which you, like most other people, fall somewhere between the extremes. If I did poorly on an exam, I should think that I've lost several percentage points in my overall grade, not that I have blown the class entirely. Or if someone appears disappointed in my behavior or performance, I should think that I have upset them in this instance, not that our relationship is over.

It is important to avoid emotionally front-loading ourselves. Instead, we should use descriptive language when assessing our situations. Instead of saying "I'm a disappointment," say "I could have done better here." Where you might say "this is the worst possible outcome," say "this could have gone better in certain respects." The goal is to express facts instead of feeling, to describe and analyze the situation instead of reacting to it. As Marcus Aurelius ponders in book twelve of his *Meditations*,

"I have often wondered how it is that every man loves himself more than all the rest of men, but yet sets less value on his own opinion of himself than on the opinion of others. If then a god or a wise teacher should present himself to a man and bid him to think of nothing and to design nothing which he would not express as soon as he conceived it, he could not endure it even for a single day. So much more respect have we to what our neighbors shall think of us than to what we shall think of ourselves."[20]

We should also examine the consequences of what we feel and do, both in the short and long term. There are pros and cons to everything we engage in. What are they? Does it serve us to lose our temper? What about denigrating ourselves? And if so, to what degree? We'll see later that the Stoics think it is never right to lose one's temper. Will you behave more rationally if you are emotionally excited? How might that affect other people or your own dispositions?

Finally, when should "should" and "ought" be used? Is an action commended or denounced in the power of you or another person? If not, they should be avoided. Further, if you or another person have some obligation, is there a conflicting obligation that overrides it? Maybe, in the case of other people, they weigh value differently than you. Is what you or they ought to do a universal value, or is it a cultural, societal, or religious preference? As Emperor Marcus Aurelius says in his *Meditations* book seven,

"When a man has done thee any wrong, immediately consider with what opinion about good or evil he has done wrong. For when thou hast seen this, thou wilt pity him, and wilt neither wonder nor be angry. For either thou thyself thinkest the same

---

20   Marcus Aurelius, *Meditations,* book twelve

thing to be good that he does or another thing of the same kind. It is thy duty then to pardon him. But if thou dost not think such things to be good or evil, thou wilt more readily be well disposed to him who is in error."[21]

This is not to say that there aren't universal values, or that right and wrong are relative, but that there are situations in which we confuse concrete duties with personal or group opinion. If you understand your own values and the values of others against the background of encompassing ethical theories, you may find that what you or they "should" do is really a matter of divergent moral premises.

Philosophical CBT, of course, extends well beyond what I've said here, with a wealth of specialized techniques and diagnosis, but I hope to have adequately covered the basics. If you have a particular problem, a pattern of reoccurring thoughts or behaviors, seeking a specialist in cognitive behavioral therapy will provide a wealth of tools with which to address them. And incorporating treatment with a Stoic mindset, introducing a new attitude toward life as a whole, can be a robust and long-lasting solution. You don't have to fight this battle alone.

---

[21]   Marcus Aurelius, *Meditations*, book seven

STOICISM AND THE EMOTIONS

It is no coincidence that cognitive behavioral therapy, inspired by ancient philosophy, puts a lot of emphasis on our emotional responses. Stoicism in general, and especially the doctrine of control, views our responses as central to human flourishing. But it is a mistake to think the Stoics, true to our modern use of their name, are resigned or emotionless. A Stoic disposition requires mastery over one's emotions, not abandonment. In this chapter, we'll take a look at what emotional mastery entails, how we fall short, and what Stoicism can teach us about emotional temperance.

Epictetus in his Discourses says Stoics are trained to act virtuously through the concepts of "appropriate action" and "discipline of action." Appropriate action concerns what we choose and avoid in our familial and social interactions. Discipline of action concerns what we choose and avoid in ourselves, what desires and habits we allow ourselves to cultivate. Both require emotional attachment to some extent, whether for others or for ourselves. Both also require that these attachments are grounded in good judgment. Stoics, ancient and modern, think that affection for one's close friends and family, for one's country, and for the whole of humanity, is natural. This expanded sphere of concern, and our resulting social wealth protect us from becoming too attached to one person or a few people. We can accept these emotions while remembering that those we care for may not live up to our expectations, that they may disappoint us. What others do is outside of our control, but we need not for that reason be indifferent to their well-being.

There is a difference between apatheia (Stoic resilience) and insensitivity. The former means one is not vulnerable to their emotions. They do not rule over us. Cicero says that the latter, insensitivity or lacking all emotion, is among the most debased ways of living. Even animals exhibit kinship and emotional attachment. By eschewing all attachment, not only are we not living up to our nature as humans, we are below animals. He says that in such a state we are more akin to a tree or a rock. Seneca further says that there can be no virtue for someone like this. To be courageous, to have self-discipline, one needs to exercise fortitude. But there is no fortitude if the challenge one is confronted with is in no way difficult. Ridding oneself of all emotions is not mastery of emotions. If feeling were to return, the insensitive person would in no way be prepared, would not have the judgment or the habits needed to overcome them. They were never confronted by an obstacle whose overcoming strengthened them, were never in a rough patch by which they could develop calluses.

Cognitive Behavioral Therapy inherited its diagnosis of the source of unhealthy emotions from Stoicism. In Stoicism, these emotions are created by irrational responses to adversity, whether overvaluing what is not in our control or desiring what is not possible. The goal is not to distance yourself from your emotions, but to identify their sources, the beliefs upon which they are founded, and replace them with new, healthy beliefs.

In Stoicism, there are also both healthy and unhealthy negative emotions. Negative in this context does not mean bad, but unpleasant, sad, or painful. Healthy negative emotions motivate us to make a change, to pursue virtue or to alter our perceptions. At the very least, they push us to avoid outcomes that could otherwise debilitate us. In place of anxiety, an unhealthy negative emotion, we might experience concern or worry. Sadness, grief, and mourning are all healthy and, opposed to depression, motivate us to overcome our circumstances or put what we have lost to rest psychologically.

Anger has a special place in the Stoic cannon. Unlike sadness or fear, anger is never permissible for the Stoics. The Stoics think that there are three components to anger. First, the perception of being wronged. This might happen when someone talks down to you, ignores you, insults you, or in any other way diminishes you. The second component is the feeling that the wrong is undeserved. If someone talks down to me or slights me after I've messed up, I might be more inclined to feel guilty or sad unless I somehow twist their words or actions so they appear to me to be uncalled for. Finally, the angry person must have the desire to retaliate. In other words, I want to "balance" the scales, to get back at them, to diminish them in kind and bring them down to my level.

We should guard ourselves especially against adopting the anger of others. If someone is angry with you, if they're attacking you verbally, giving you the cold shoulder, or defaming you in the presence of others, you may very well become angry in turn. Remember Epictetus' words from his *Enchiridion*,

"When any person harms you, or speaks badly of you, remember that he acts or speaks from a supposition of its being his duty. Now, it is not possible that he should follow what appears right to you, but what appears so to himself. Therefore, if he judges from a wrong appearance, he is the person hurt, since he too is the person deceived. For if anyone should suppose a true proposition to be false, the proposition is not hurt, but he who is deceived about it. Setting out, then, from these principles, you will meekly bear a person who reviles you, for you will say upon every occasion, 'It seemed so to him.'"[22]

In this case, you might think you're justified. After all, the other person injured themselves; they did not show patience in dealing with you, so why should you be patient with them? This kind of emotional spillover—from another person—is all too common in relationships and work environments. But is it really sound to

---

22   Epictetus, *Enchiridion*

argue that they deserve to suffer in the same way they're causing you to suffer?

Epictetus says that there is never a cause to get angry. The only way another person could "injure" us is by attacking or debasing some external, whether it be our property, our bodies, or our reputation. But none of these are really ours, we do not control them. What we do control is our internal lives, our faculty of choice, and it is that very faculty that is injured when we lose our temper. By getting angry, we skew our judgment and sacrifice our discipline. This kind of debasement is not something any other person or any external circumstance can do to us. We bring this upon ourselves.

Anger tends toward a kind of mission creep. When angry, we often misjudge what is and isn't in our control. First, we misjudge whether or not the source of our anger really injured us, whether it in any way diminished our inner lives. Second, we misjudge whether or not becoming angry will harm the object of our anger, whether person or thing. Outwardly, we can insult them or damage their person or property, but they themselves can only be harmed if they allow it. Even in this latter case, it is never we ourselves who are doing the harm.

The discussion of anger brings us back around to the preferred Stoic method of combating emotional malfeasance, shifting perspective. In this case, is what we're angry about really under our control? If my friend goes a few weeks without talking to me, but it's clear that they're still talking to others, that is their choice, painful though it might be for me. Instead of lessening the pain their indifference causes me, I'm only adding to it by seething, by dwelling on their actions. And if I decide to curse them out, to yell, to make a scene, is it more or less likely that they will want to remain friends? I must show discipline (*ascesis*) and endure their actions, remembering that they are also free subjects, capable of making decisions with regard to their inner and outer life, even if their actions disappoint me.

What is the Stoic approach to fear, and how can we master our fears using Stoic methods? The Stoics identify two types of fears. The fist kind is a knee-jerk response to certain stimuli, like being startled or disgusted by an unexpected event or sensation. The ancient Stoics called this *propatheia*, pre-emotions. They are often physiological responses, as unmediated as one blocking his or her face when a ball is thrown at it. It is after we experience these surprises that we judge their cause positive or negative, good or bad. If, after experiencing and reflecting upon it, we judge that the thing responsible is a true evil or harm, we experience real fear.

The Stoics emphasize that real fear is a choice or a judgment we consciously make. It is up to us whether we assert or deny that a thing is truly frightening, and further how to respond to it. If we do not assent that a thing is frightening or threatening, we will not be afraid. The Stoics do not, therefore, suggest that we eschew all fears, that we become totally fearless or insensible to danger. Rather, the Stoics recommend we replace fear with caution, *eulabeia*. This state does not combine worry and anxiety with fear, but instead with conscientiousness and curiosity. Instead of being shuttered away from our fears, we are called to become intimate with them, too, through a thorough acquaintance with their origins and functioning, master them. Rather than a disposition open to recklessness, the Stoic response is informed resignation, such that we accept our fears to defeat them.

To conclude our discussion of the emotions, before moving on to Stoic exercises, consider what it means to master them. Grief, anger, and anxiety tend to, when unrestrained, become habits. We can feel restrained and even helpless when we eschew them. If someone diminishes me and I don't retaliate, I may feel that I'm being trampled upon. If I do not express my sadness at some loss, if I do not let myself go, I can feel bottled up, repressed. Remember the words of Marcus Aurelius from book twelve of his *Meditations*:

"When thou art troubled about anything, thou hast forgotten this, that all things happen according to the universal nature; and forgotten this, that a man's wrongful act is nothing to thee; and further thou hast forgotten this, that everything which happens, always happened so and will happen so, and now happens so everywhere; forgotten this too, how close is the kinship between a man and the whole human race, for it is a community, not of a little blood or seed, but of intelligence. And thou hast forgotten this too, that every man's intelligence is a god, and is an efflux of the deity; and forgotten this, that nothing is a man's own, but that his child and his body and his very soul came from the deity; forgotten this, that everything is opinion; and lastly thou hast forgotten that every man lives the present time only, and loses only this." [23]

To a certain extent, these are correct interpretations. But consider that restrained grief, grief that is healthy and directed toward some end, is more productive toward healing than a spiral into depression. Similarly, anger spirals out of control. It is like a fire that consumes everything, both its object and us. It is more productive toward proving that we are not as small as fate or another person would have us feel to hold our temper, to rise above subservience to passion. In both cases, retaining our judgment secures our needs better than our emotional response. Think of the words of Emperor Marcus Aurelius, from book five of his *Meditations*,

"Art thou angry with him whose armpits stink? Art thou angry with him whose mouth smells foul? What good will this danger do thee? He has such a mouth, he has such arm-pits: it is

---

23   Marcus Aurelius, *Meditations*, book twelve

necessary that such an emanation must come from such things- but the man has reason, it will be said, and he is able, if he takes pain, to discover wherein he offends- I wish thee well of thy discovery."[24]

A life of emotional mastery is no more unrestrained than it is insensible. It is in this mean between the extremes, in addressing what we feel rationally, that we satisfy those aims which our emotions demand. This is a life of engaged contentment, the core of which vigilance and exercise.

---

[24] Marcus Aurelius, *Meditations,* book five

Outer Troubles; Preventative Measures in Stoicism

What we choose and what we avoid says a lot about who we are. It broadcasts our priorities, whether concerning which people we prefer, or which objects. It also determines when our quality of life will be disrupted. If we attach ourselves to the wrong things, to externals, positive or negative, we open ourselves to suffering and misfortune. A key Stoic concept is, therefore, to steel oneself against negative circumstances, to win the battle for our inner life before it's fought. This chapter focuses on preventive Stoic exercises, those actions you can take before you're faced with a dilemma. We will examine the methods and the mental states, many over two thousand years old, that great Stoics like Epictetus, Marcus Aurelius, Seneca, and Musonius Rufus taught and used, and, through example, apply these circumstances to modern life.

Marcus Aurelius championed a technique today referred to as "the view from above." Therein he recommended a kind of withdrawn attitude toward your circumstances, one that views particular events in relation to the whole of creation. We should strive, Marcus thinks, to rid ourselves of those useless things which disturb us. If we see how rapidly the world changes, how short the individual's life is and how vast the passage of time was before we were born and will be after we die, we can protect ourselves from trifles before they occur.

The view from above is partly related to the doctrine of control discussed in an earlier chapter. The aim of both is to fix in our minds those things worth our concern. What should I fear from death? Is it not the case that every person before has died, and that every person will die, and that eventually, the whole human race will be extinct? I'll let Marcus speak for himself. In book two of his *Meditations*, he says,

"Every moment think steadily as a Roman and a man to do what thou hast in hand with perfect and simple dignity, and feeling of affection, and freedom, and justice; and to give thyself relief from all other thoughts. And thou wilt give thyself relief, if thou doest every act of thy life as if it were the last, laying aside all carelessness and passionate aversion from the commands of reason, and all hypocrisy, and self-love, and discontent with the portion which has been given to thee. Thou seest how few the things are, the which if a man lays hold of, he is able to live a life which flows in quiet, and is like the existence of the gods; for the gods on their part will require nothing more from him who observes these things."[25]

My suffering, then, and my fear of death, is minuscule when considered in relation to the whole of existence. Marcus

---

[25] Marcus Aurelius, *Meditations*, book two

challenges us to take this view toward death so we can live with purpose. If even my death is a minuscule event, how much smaller is that irritation I felt in the office last week? Was it worth dwelling on for days?

When we get up in the morning, Marcus says, we should remember exactly how small we are. Remember that we will have to face people no less small, to suffer any number of indignities, and to conduct ourselves with poise. In book two of his *Meditations*, Marcus says,

"Begin the morning by saying to thyself, I shall meet with the busy-body, the ungrateful, arrogant, deceitful, envious, unsocial. All these things happen to them by reason of their ignorance of what is good and evil. But I who have seen the nature of the good that it is beautiful, and of the bad that it is ugly, and the nature of him who does wrong, that it is akin to me, not only of the same blood or seed, but that it participates in the same intelligence and the same portion of the divinity, I can neither be injured by any of them, for no one can fix on me what is ugly, nor can I be angry with my kinsman, nor hate him, For we are made for co-operation, like feet, like hands, like eyelids, like the rows of the upper and lower teeth. To act against one another then is contrary to nature; and it is acting against one another to be vexed and to turn away."[26]

If we keep in mind that those who vex us face the same fate we do, we can accept whatever minor victory they perceive for themselves when they diminish us. Even the highest, most powerful people cannot escape death, they will also be swept aside in the long-run. It, therefore, matters even less to what degree someone's pettiness elevates them. They are not as important as great people, and even great people are not important at all. Marcus Aurelius counsels us about such people when he says:

"Besides wherein hast thou been injured? For thou wilt find that no one among those against whom thou art irritated has done anything by which thy mind could be made worse; but that which is evil to thee and harmful has its foundation only in the mind. And what harm is done or what is there strange, if the man who has not been instructed does the acts of an uninstructed man? Consider whether thou shouldst not rather blame thyself, because thou didst not expect such a man to err in such a way. For thou hadst means given thee by thy reason to suppose that it was likely that he would commit this error, and yet thou hast forgotten and art amazed that he has erred."[27]

---

26 Marcus Aurelius, *Meditations*, book two
27 ibid

There is another technique whose center is a recognition of our finitude. Seneca says that it is important to love the people in our circle, but we must remember that they are not ours to keep. Fate brought them into our lives, and fate will eventually take them from us. We must, therefore, while loving them, remember that they will not always be with us. We must practice our love for them such that we take full advantage of our limited time together. This exercise is double-edged: First we should take joy and comfort in them where we can, second, we should limit our enjoyment, not become singularly attached or fixated on spending time with them.

How does this look in practice? My grandmother is very old now. In comparison to me, her time is short. But what time she does have she dedicates to us, to her family. Not a day goes by where she isn't visited by at least one of us, and often it's several of us together. This is the kind of behavior about which Seneca speaks. We should treat all those we care about as though their time is short because it is. In doing so we not only maximize what little time we have, we also prepare for the end of that time.

Another kind of exercise, also recommended by Marcus Aurelius, is premeditating evil. Imagine the worst that can happen during your day, your year, or your lifetime. Imagine yourself stricken with poverty or illness, or imagine that your endeavors fail. What do these misfortunes feel like? What will you do to confront them? Marcus says we should move our minds toward overcoming them; we should imagine ourselves enduring disappointments and setbacks, and then growing in spite of them. We should also imagine ourselves shifting our focus back toward the good, toward virtue, while wrapped in despair. As Marcus says in book four of his *Meditations*,

"Men seek retreats for themselves, houses in the country, seashores, and mountains; and thou too art wont to desire such things very much. But this is altogether a mark of the most common sort of men, for it is in thy power whenever thou shalt choose to retire into thyself. For nowhere either with more quiet or more freedom from trouble does a man retire than into his own soul, particularly when he has within him such thoughts that by looking into them he is immediately in perfect tranquility; and I affirm that tranquillity is nothing else than the good ordering of the mind."[28]

We might draw an analogy to physical exercise here. Some people find it helpful to, before a workout, visualize what the workout will involve, the discomfort they'll experience, and their desire to quit half-way, to prepare themselves mentally. They also imagine the end of the workout and what benefits they'll reap after their routine is over. When the time comes to start the routine, they've already prepped themselves for the strain, they

---

28   Marcus Aurelius, *Meditations,* book four

have anticipated every aspect of their training, including the desire to quit. What Marcus recommends is also the anticipation of a strenuous workout, but for the mind and for our willpower. This is another good exercise to try early in the morning, before work or school, especially when you anticipate less than pleasant people. Imagine your goal, whether it be passing the class, receiving your paycheck, or just making it home afterward.

Related to this defensive technique is the exercise of writing Stoic aphorisms. When you start your day, or even before you get out of bed in the morning, write down a Stoic saying that you think will be helpful for what's to come. Commit that saying to memory, then write a short summary of it in your own words, and a bit about how you think it applies to your situation. Carry the journal, paper, or book in which you wrote the saying with you and, when you can, write down the times throughout the day where it was pertinent, and whether or not you think you lived up to your interpretation of it. Then, at the end of the day, review what you wrote. Upon reflection, did your original interpretation of the passage prove true? If so, where did you meet the challenge it issued? Where did you fail? If not, how would you alter your interpretation to better accord with your experience? Write these meditations down and refer to them again the next time that particular piece of wisdom is relevant.

Try having a conversation with yourself from the future. Say you think of yourself at the end of your Stoic exercises. Think of the kinds of qualities you would like yourself to have, the kinds of virtues you would like yourself to exercise, the kind of disposition you would like yourself to cultivate. If you, as a time traveler, went forward to meet this version of yourself and ask about your current troubles, what would that you say? What advice would they give on how to deal with the annoying colleague, the stressful job, or the frightening turn of events? Bringing these concrete situations to the ideal you is akin to the next exercise, which I consider a superior version because it challenges you to not just think of a better version of yourself but of a virtuous person tout court, exercising your understanding of the virtues at the same time that it calls you to practical, meditative activity. Which version you prefer, however, may be different, so I offer both and leave it open for you to decide.

Let's consider a final exercise in the anticipatory framework, then, examining values. Imagine the qualities of a virtuous person. In what sorts of situations are they kind, philanthropic, well-tempered? How would they endure the challenges awaiting you? Now imagine the vicious person. Where do they fall short? How would they handle your challenges? Write down some key qualities you think describe these people. These are your guiding attributes. As Epictetus says in his *Enchiridion*,

"Immediately prescribe some character and form of conduce to yourself, which you may keep both alone and in company."[29]

We can also heed the words of Marcus Aurelius in book six of his Meditations when he says:

"When thou wishest to delight thyself, think of the virtues of those who live with thee; for instance, the activity of one, and the modesty of another, and the liberality of a third, and some other good quality of a fourth. For nothing delights so much as the examples of the virtues, when they are exhibited in the morals of those who live with us and present themselves in abundance, as far as is possible. Wherefore we must keep them before us."

Through the day, take note of situations in which you tend toward the virtuous or the viscous person. Your goal is to learn what kind of situations you should meet and what kind you should avoid. Further, for those situations that test you or in which you tend toward viscous qualities—toward intemperance, cowardice, or injustice—take note of how you fall short, and suggest for yourself what you can do to overcome these hardships. Once you've finished your day, flip the page, start a new entry, or even grab a new notebook if you must! You should treat each day as a new experience, as a new opportunity to meet your goals, and you should also make a new list and set new goals as your thoughts evolve. And when you're ready, review

---

29   Epictetus, *Enchiridion*

your progress over the last week or month. You'll be surprised at how far you can develop in a short time.

"Preventative measures are all good," you might tell me, "but what about when I am in the moment?" In the end, the exercise of virtue comes down to a moment-to-moment, situation-to-situation decisions. In the next chapter, let's look at some Stoic exercises for dealing with our problems as they arise, and for reflecting upon them after they have passed.

Stoic Discomfort

The Stoics see one's approach to misfortune as crucial to a life of tranquility. Suffering can take on many forms, from damaged property to damaged relationships, to death. Our poor circumstances, the Stoics think, breed opportunities to practice virtue. It is a central tenant of Stoic practice that one is strengthened whenever they handle unfortunate situations in a thoughtful and disciplined way. Of course, one does not seek misfortune for the sake of practice, but it is not necessary to anyway. Even minor slights, petty disagreements, and minute irritants can help us develop our habits and our faculty of choice in a way that is in accordance with nature, that contributes to human flourishing. In this chapter I will discuss daily discomforts in the context of Stoic practice, to show you ways you can cope with unfortunate events, both great and small.

Imagine you are in your favorite restaurant, about to enjoy your favorite dish. You smell the seasoning, admire the color, feel the texture, savor the taste. And when the meal is done, you are left wanting more; you are even upset that it did not last longer. So what do you do? You pay your check and leave the restaurant. But you enjoyed yourself so much, how could you possibly walk away without ordering more? There could be many practical reasons. The dish is expensive, you are already full, you have an appointment. But another reason is that you know, fate permitting, this isn't the last time you'll taste good food. You enjoyed the meal, but you are not singularly attached to that experience at that time. You don't feel an immediate need to repeat it.

This above attitude is akin to how the Stoics think we should treat enjoyments. When we experience any pleasure, we should not be carried away by it. We should not allow ourselves to lose control of our emotions. Their reasoning is twofold. First, they think a resigned attitude toward pleasure is also practiced for when we confront pain. Epictetus says in his *Enchiridion*,

"If you are struck by the appearance of any promised pleasure, guard yourself against being hurried away by it; but let the affair wait for your leisure, and procure yourself some delay. Then bring to your mind both points of time: that in which you will enjoy the pleasure, and that in which you will repent and reproach yourself after you have enjoyed it; and set before you, in opposition to these, how you will be glad and applaud yourself if you abstain. And even though it should appear to you a seasonable gratification, take heed that its enticing, and agreeable and attractive force may not subdue you; but set in opposition to this how much better it is to be conscious of having gained so great a victory."[30]

---

30   Epictetus, *Enchiridion*

If, after all, you cannot control yourself during enjoyment, how can you expect to enjoy yourself when you're suffering, when it may be more difficult to maintain discipline? Emperor Marcus Aurelius speaks of the temptation of sleep in particular. In book five of his *Meditations*, he says,

"In the morning when thou risest unwillingly, let this thought be present- I am rising to the work of a human being. Why then am I dissatisfied if I am going to do the things for which I exist and for which I was brought into the world? Or have I been made for this, to lie in the bed-clothes and keep myself warm?- But this is more pleasant.- Dost thou exist then to take thy pleasure, and not at all for action or exertion? Dost thou does not see the little plants, the little birds, the ants, the spiders, the bees working together to put in order their several parts of the universe? And art thou unwilling to do the work of a human being, and dost thou do not make haste to do that which is according to thy nature?"[31]

Second, they think you are thereby asserting control over your emotions. Epictetus says that we should make our impressions wait for us, rather than the other way around. Know that you are just fine without experiencing any given sensation, that you have control over it, and you will find it becomes easier to restrain yourself when it matters.

---

31   Marcus Aurelius, *Meditations*, book five

But how do we measure when restraint is appropriate and to what degree it is appropriate? Epictetus says we should measure our actions within the context of our relationships and our situation. If your sibling harms you, you do not cut ties with them, not only because you might one day need a kidney, but also because familial relationships are within our closest circle of concern. These are the people most important to us. But if an acquaintance wrongs you, though you should not lose your temper or concern yourself with actions that are not your own, you are under no obligation to continue interacting with that person. In fact, if they prove to be a continual irritant, and if they themselves are vicious, the Stoics recommend you cease contact. In both situations, your response is in proportion to the care you can and should be expected to show toward that person. Similarly, when dealing with pleasures and pains, act in accordance with sound judgment, in proportion to the impression under question.

The Stoics call upon us to live consistently. If you think someone else should behave a certain way, whether it is by showing patience, restraining their fear, or being just in their exchanges with others, ask yourself whether or not you are also living up to that principle. If you are not, or if there are situations in which you have fallen short in the past, do not expect another person to be better than you are. By looking at people in the context of our own abilities, we temper our expectations and eschew pain arising from their shortcomings.

I think the best way to ensure your expectations align with your abilities, and with what can be expected from others, is to engage in Stoic meditations. Meditation for the Stoics is not like it is in Buddhism; it does not involve clearing your mind and accepting impressions as they arise and pass away. Stoic meditation is an active process in which you evaluate your actions and ideas, dig through them for those attitudes you will keep and those you will discard. We can split the list of questions you should ask yourself into two, one following Epictetus' example, the other following Seneca's.

Before looking at the kinds of questions each of these thinkers would have you ask, consider a broader inquiry. Ask yourself what you did wrong today. Which of your actions do you accept, which do you condemn? Also, ask what virtue and strength you've shown today. Were your actions consistent with your nature as a rational subject? What can you do to realign them? Finally, ask what you can do better. You may not be correcting follies here, but looking for situations in which you could have exercised virtue, in which you could have gone beyond neutral activity.

Once you have answered these general questions, consider the kinds of questions Epictetus would ask himself. Did you go wrong in any way that hinders your serenity or personal flourishing? Did you attribute blame to those who did not deserve it, or take umbrage at some event or circumstance not under your control? What did you do that was antisocial, inconsiderate, or unfriendly? Did you, to your fullest extent, exercise justice with respect to others? If not, what duties did you abrogate in your relationships? What effect do you think your actions will have on others, and, in the long term, what damage have you done to yourself? These questions behind you, let us not turn to Seneca, who asks a similar, but distinct, set of questions.

Seneca draws his questions from the meditations of Sextus Empericus. Before he would close his eyes and fall asleep, the latter would ask himself three things. First, which of your evils have you cured today? This question was a call to account for moral development, a measure of his progress toward virtuous living. Second, which of your vices have you fought? In other words, which of your bad habits did you target, and where did you succeed or fail in overcoming them. Finally, how are you better? Is there any sense in which you have improved yourself and, if not, how can you change your behaviors to make a difference in your character tomorrow?

If you give yourself an honest account, you can take, to what extent it is possible, an objective view of yourself and your failings. But it is also important to praise yourself when you do well. To do so is to treat yourself both as a friend and a wise counselor. The idea of these questions, and of taking a Stoic view toward your failings, is to apply the theoretical aspects of Stoic doctrine, in order to live a fuller and more consistent life. A life worthy of human nature.

APATHEIA — STOIC INNER PEACE

For the Stoics, the center of eudaimonia, human flourishing, is apatheia, being without passions. I have said before that this, despite being the Hellenistic root of our English word apathy, does not mean indifference or insensitivity. Apatheia Is to be thought of in relation to our earlier discussion of emotional mastery. For the Stoics, it is the name of that state that arises when one has been thoroughly dyed in virtue. And, crucially for us, it is the end goal of Stoic training and exercises. In a word, the good life is one in which the state of apatheia is the core of right choices in ethical action.

When the Stoics use the term passion, they do not mean only emotion. To be more precise, the Stoic passions, as we saw in the chapter on CBT, can be either healthy or unhealthy. Examples of unhealthy passions include fear, pain, pleasure, and cravings. Healthy passions include caution, discretion, delight and willing. Caution and discretion are the opposites of fear, delight is the opposite of pleasure, willing is the opposite of craving. Pain does not have an opposite that is still a "passion" in the Stoic sense of the term. As you can see, the Stoic passions are not quite emotions. It is more correct to say that they are affections of the soul.

The passions are in a way instinctive reactions, the experience of which we cannot avoid. They result from a kind of assent given to impressions. We saw an example of this assent with respect to fear, where the initial shock of an encounter became fear when one reflected upon and chose to designate it an evil. It is not correct to identify fear as the initial fight-or-flight response to a perceived danger. Once it is or has become subject to your control, once it is presented to your soul, to your faculty of choice, then it is a passion in the proper sense.

Pain considered as a passion for the Stoics in a sense mirrors the Epicurean meaning of the word. For the Epicureans, pains were not just the feeling of discomfort, but a feeling whose origin was in a choice, specifically the failure to choose to avoid something. For the Stoics, too, pain is not just the feeling of hurt or injury, but also an irrational expectation. To be sure cutting oneself on a piece of glass is a pain in part of its sense, just as being startled is part of the meaning is fear. But these initial or involuntary reactions do not capture the full meanings of the words and for that reason the Stoics the limited senses of the words from those senses which involve what is fully us, our decision making core. As Emperor Marcus Aurelius says in book nine of his *Meditations*,

"Thou canst remove out of the way many useless things among those which disturb thee, for they lie entirely in thy opinion; and thou wilt then gain for thyself ample space by comprehending the whole universe in thy mind, and by contemplating the eternity of time, and observing the rapid change of every several thing, how short is the time from birth to dissolution, and the illimitable time before birth as well as the equally boundless time after dissolution."[32]

Apatheia is a state in which these unhealthy passions are turned on their heads. In the examples given above, one who is affected by Stoic apatheia, instead of experiencing fear, experiences a sense caution. One who would experience an intense craving, an irrational striving for something mistakenly judged as good, instead experiences wishing, a rational desire for virtue. One who would be subject to pleasure, an irrational elation over something that is actually not worth choosing, would instead experience joy or delight, a rational elation over virtue. By their very phrasing, "rational elation over virtue," etc., you can see that these dispositions are a kind of habituation, an inner discipline or well-developed faculty of choice that governs both our reactions to these passions and those objects that excite our passions to begin with.

Apatheia also yields a second state, one at which the Epicureans in their pursuit of pleasure aimed directly, ataraxia. Ataraxia means "imperturbability" or literally being without trouble or tranquility. For the Epicureans, this meant that, through prudent living and correct choices, one relieved themselves of pain, this being for them the greatest sort of pleasure or the limit of

---

[32] Marcus Aurelius, *Meditations,* book nine

pleasure. For the Stoics, it means living a life in accordance with one's nature, which means a life of virtue. Such a life is directed toward its aims—it accomplishes its goals and is thereby brought into tranquility, even if that tranquility leads one through what are otherwise discomforts like engaging in social or political life, an aspect of human experience that the Epicureans recommended we avoid at all cost.

This brings us at last to one final idea, that of Stoic cosmopolitanism. Indeed, if there is any rational opposite of misdirected passion in politics, it is this notion. For the Stoics, the aim of political life is securing the reproduction and improvement of public virtue. In book nine of his *Meditations*, Marcus Aurelius says:

"As thou thyself art a component part of a social system, so let every act of thine be a component part of social life. Whatever act of thine then has no reference either immediately or remotely to a social end, this tears asunder thy life, and does not allow it to be one, and it is of the nature of a mutiny, just as when in a popular assembly a man acting by himself stands apart from the general agreement."[33]

Public virtue is the opposite of private virtue in the sense that the latter has only the well-being of the self as its end while the former sees the exercise of virtue in context. The case is easy

---

33   Marcus Aurelius, *Meditations*, book nine

enough with justice. When one engages with others such that obligations are upheld, and when this becomes a general rule, society is more cohesive. What of courage or temperance? Is society not improved when individuals endure difficult circumstances and take only what satisfies their needs? When virtue is directed toward civic improvement when philosophical practice is also political practice, the individual benefits as well as the polity.

Here too Stoic practice meets its pedagogical ends. By living a life according to virtue, by developing apatheia as a disposition, one serves as a living example of their theoretical commitments. And this active life of spreading philosophy, as we saw at the very beginning of this book, is the aim of philosophy as a discipline. Mastery of the passions, then, is a necessary condition for the spreading of Stoic ideas, insofar as those ideas flourish when they are lived. Remember here the words of Epictetus from his *Enchiridion*:

"And, if anyone tells you that you know nothing, and you are not nettled at it, then you may be sure that you have begun your business. For sheep don't throw up the grass to show the shepherds how much they have eaten; but, inwardly digesting their food, they outwardly produce wool and milk. Thus, therefore, do you likewise not show theorems to the unlearned, but the actions produced by them after they have been digested."[34]

---

[34] Epictetus, *Enchiridion*

Conclusion

Stoicism as an ethical system brings together logic, physics, ethics, and psychology to paint a picture of the whole human being. I hope I have, in this book, presented its ideas in a clear, digestible format pleasing to both the eyes and the mind.

It is no secret that Stoicism's survival, its flourishing, and its rebirth are due to its malleability and the applicability of its doctrines. Epictetus says often that it is not enough to know Stoic doctrine, one must also practice, to develop habits, if they want to master its ideas and understand it in practice.

When I first encountered Stoicism, it was as an undergraduate in college. At the time I had very little interest in philosophy as a whole outside of those goals which served my ego—having the upper hand in arguments, justifying my beliefs, and adding another chip to my shoulder. Stoicism did not at the time appeal to me. I should have heeded Epictetus' words when he says in the *Enchiridion*,

"Never call yourself a philosopher, nor talk a great deal among the unlearned about theorems, but act conformably to them. Thus, at an entertainment, don't talk how persons ought to eat, but eat as you ought. For remember that in this manner Socrates also universally avoided all ostentation. And when persons came to him and desired to be recommended by him to philosophers, he took and- recommended them, so well did he bear being overlooked."[35]

It was several years, and a bit more engagement with philosophy, before the value of Stoicism became evident. Its treatment of the human being as a whole, engaging both the nature of the mind and its relationship to social responsibility, is not unique in philosophy, but no other individual philosophy can claim to have had such a far-reaching impact on the lives of people not wading through the theoretical reeds.

I think it is this accessibility, deeply connected to the breadth of its applicability, that explains its success. Whether dealing with trouble in the workplace, at home, or in one's own heart, Stoicism is a well of wisdom whose wealth has been drawn consistently for thousands of years. Whether considering what one controls, or how to apply what is controlled and what is not (for example the relationship between what is in our power and what is assigned to us as a duty, like the rearing of our children), or the application of virtue in ethical life.

The Stoic sage is untroubled by that which they cannot control, but also capable of boundless compassion for friends and family, country, and the whole of humanity. This principle of Stoic concern is called cosmopolitanism; it is intimately connected with the idea that we are citizens of the world. Further, it draws

---

[35] Epictetus, *Enchiridion*

upon the idea of Divine Fire we discussed earlier. We are all sparks of creation, the force that moves all of creation also moves us. It is for this reason that we must recognize ourselves and our motivations as situated in an interconnected whole, one damaged when we fail to treat one another with respect and compassion.

Stoic compassion is a central theme, as maybe you've gleaned from this book. As I've said before, the Stoics are the opposite of insensible, despite this being one of their popular reputations. Their doctrines are infused with care for those who deserve it, charity for those who need it, and understanding for those who fail in their responsibilities. With respect to duty, especially duties concerning those in our care, the Stoics entreat us to show due attention, but also warn us against passion. This is not an idle doctrine. What care is appropriate to the maintenance of what has been loaned to us by fortune is both the limit of our attachment and the appropriate attitude to see it preserved. Passion, on the other hand, is the cousin of exuberance and overreaction and, even in the

It is said that the great Emperor Marcus Aurelius was a fortress of these attitudes. Can you imagine, the most powerful man in the world, one with absolute authority over life and death in the entire known world, living a life in service to those beneath him? We live with minor temptations. Whether or not to cheat on our taxes, to shoplift a beverage, to cheat on our spouse. How much more must this temptation be for one with absolute impunity? Who could get away with any crime, have any woman, appropriate all the wealth in the world if he so desired? We know that other Roman emperors were not able to resist their temptations. But it is evidence of the power of Stoic ideas that The Stoic Emperor would be the superior of those that preceded him and those that followed.

We can follow his example. If he, with all his might, could resist his temptations, I think we have hope. In truth, what Stoic doctrines ask of us is not grand. After all, many of us already record our thoughts in journals, logs, and stories. In the west, we are obsessed with data. Everything from our heart rate to our calorie intake, to the number of steps we take is already recorded. Recording our moral development is not too far a stretch! I think, at any rate, the information recorded is more useful than a record of the number of carbs we've consumed. As for its difficulty, we should remember the words of Epictetus from chapter twelve, book three of his *Discourses*. There he says:

"Everything, which is difficult and dangerous is not suitable for practice; but that is suitable which conduces to the working out of that which is proposed to us as a thing to be worked out. To live with desire and aversion, free from restraint. And what is this? Neither to be disappointed in that which you desire nor to fall into anything which you would avoid. Toward this object, then, exercise ought to tend. For, since it is not possible to have your desire not disappointed and your aversion free from falling into that which you would avoid, great and constant practice you must know that if you allow your desire and aversion to turn to things which are not within the power of the will, you will neither have your desire capable of attaining your object, nor your aversion free from the power of avoiding that which you would avoid."[36]

Just like the other information we keep track of, there is a wealth of opportunity for social engagement in Stoic self-evaluation. Already numerous groups, blogs, and communities have formed online and around the world filled with like-minded people focused on the improvement of themselves and their communities. Modern Stoicism is alive and growing. This book, too, is an entry in a revived philosophical movement. I hope you use it as a gateway. Though I've tried to cover all aspects of Stoicism to some extent, each topic touched on here is far more complex than I could field between these pages. By engaging with others, by sharing your experiences and your failings, you will uncover a mountain of practical advice aimed both at expanding on the ideas discussed here and on troubleshooting them. As with anything, Stoicism takes work. The dispositions outlined here may be at times difficult to wrap your head around, at other times their applicability might not be

---

[36] Epictetus, *Discourses,* book three, chapter twelve

immediately obvious, but studying and understanding them is preparation for possible experiences. Experiences that others have had, and that you, too, might one day encounter.

It has been a joy and a pleasure taking the plunge with you and being your guide. I hope you also enjoyed the experience. Remember that Stoicism is half theoretical, half practical. It is possible that many misunderstandings will remain even after years of study. As with any sufficiently complex philosophical theory, there is always something new to discover, some new aspect or way of reading the text to uncover. With Stoicism especially, finding these new readings will require you to live the doctrine, and also teach others. You do not, of course, have to sit down with them and go over the details of Stoic virtue. Rather, you should live Stoic teachings, and teach by example in turn. Through consistent and engaged activity, you'll not only find your own life improved but also the lives of your loved ones—both inside and out.

Bibliography

Epictetus. *The Enchiridion*. Translated by Elizabeth Carter. http://classics.mit.edu/Epictetus/epicench.html.

Aurelius, Marcus. *Meditations*. Translated by George Long. http://classics.mit.edu/Antoninus/meditations.html.

Cicero, Marcus T. *On Duties*. Translated by Cyrus R. Edmonds. New York, NY: Harper & Brothers, 1855. https://archive.org/stream/cicerosthreebook00cicerich/cicerosthreebook00cicerich_djvu.txt.

Epictetus. *Discourses*. http://classics.mit.edu/Epictetus/discourses.html.

Description

Tag line: Stoicism, one of the oldest, Western philosophical schools, has enchanted scholars and the general public alike for over two thousand years. Where some accounts of human nature and the particularly human good fall short by the reduction of human being to physical or psychical phenomena, Stoicism's power lies in engaging with the whole range of human experience, addressing rationality, emotion, piety, will, and both inner and outer impressions, each on their own terms, in language that treats each as significant in its own right.

This book is a general introduction to Stoicism that pulls no punches when faced with the more complex aspects of Stoic doctrine. Topics addressed include:

- -The history of the ancient Stoics.
- -The nature of good and evil, virtue and vice, and positive and negative externals.
- -The difference between those things in our control and those things not in our control.
- -Stoic Logic and practical reasoning.
- -Stoicism's role in the development of cognitive behavioral therapy (CBT).
- -Stoic exercises and daily practice.

- -Theology's role in Stoicism and Stoic cosmology.
- And much more!

Stoicism is an active philosophy. That means that it is not enough to know its doctrines, one must also live them, develop habits that expand on and complete their ideas in practice. Practice, therefore, is also the focus of this book. The development of the reader's inner and outer life, that they may follow their own path and discover what it means to "live life in accordance with nature."

DAILY STOIC:

DESCRIPTION

This book is a collection of Stoic sayings organized to allow daily reference and inspiration. Including quotes from Marcus Aurelius, Seneca, Epictetus, and more, the Stoic advice covered in this volume runs the gambit from personal problems, to interpersonal relationships, to advice on work and productivity, to dealing with the hand of fate.

Face the world with a new light with the help of these immortal thinkers and learn both to conquer yourself and to come to terms with those things which you cannot control.

INTRODUCTION

Season One: Winter, Revival, and Coming to Terms.

a. Stoicism and Depression – Passages concerning sadness, coping, and revitalizing yourself.
b. Deprecation and Anger – How to handle changing moods, especially the strongest one.
c. Motivation – Stoic tips for staying active.
d. Fear, Regret and New Beginnings – Overcoming discrepancies between how you saw yourself last year and how you see yourself now.

Season Two: Spring, A Time for New Beginnings

a. Relinquishing the Past – Passages on forgiveness.
b. Body Image – Stoic advice for self-perception, focusing on control (or lack thereof) of one's appetites and health.
c. Life and Living Well – Stoic passages on birth and the promise of the future.
d. What to do With Work – Advice concerning heavy workloads and positive reinforcement.
e. Open to Possibilities – What the Stoics thought about views and anticipation of the future.

Summer: Problems in The Prime of Life

   a. Relaxing: Not Just for Kids – The Stoics on leisure.
   b. On Temperament and Temperature – Stoic advice on environmental and physical stress.
   c. Living in Your Prime – How the Stoics viewed those in their prime and what to do with their vigor.

Fall: Change, Loss, and The End of Vitality

   a. The Stoics and Loss – Stoics on dealing with life changes.
   b. Being Prepared – Passages on reflecting on and preparing for shifts in fortune.
   c. Dealing with Death – The Stoics and death, personal and impersonal.

Introduction: Stoicism and the Virtuous Life

Stoicism is an ancient philosophical school that has survived and thrived across ages, circumstances, and empires. Like many ancient schools, Stoicism has its origins in Athens. It first flourished alongside the noble Academy of Plato, the secretive Aristotelian Peripatetics, and the infamous Epicurean Garden. Stoicism's founder, Zeno of Citium, is famous for having taught freely in the "Stoa Poikile" or "Painted Porch" in English, from which the school derives its name.

The Stoics embody the love of wisdom. Their emphasis is practice, is living by example, both by teaching Stoic doctrine, particularly ethics, and by being exemplars of the doctrines they teach. Collectively, they define philosophy as a kind of activity, or *askêsis* in Greek, of knowledge concerning what is beneficial. Like the Epicureans, their approach to philosophy was therapeutic. They emphasized the development of good habits through knowledge of what is and is not to be valued. They aimed to strengthen the faculty of choice, *prohairesis* in Greek, and to thereby cultivate wisdom, to create Stoic sages.

The center and aim of the Stoic life is to be in accord with nature. Remember to keep separate their idea of nature from our modern idea of it. While it's true that instinct and inheritance plays a part in their concept, they also conceive of a thing's full development as belonging to its nature. If I ask "what is the nature of this seed?" you could say "to become a tree." This would be in accord with the Stoic idea of nature; it is not just the seed's nature to be an embryo housed in a coat with its nutrients, but also to grow into a tree in the right conditions. On the other hand, a person might be inclined to lie, cheat, and steal because of an evolutionary adaptation, and this may be the nature of an undeveloped person, but it is also within their nature to grow beyond that, to develop rationally and morally. Just as a seed that does not grow into a tree might be said to have failed with respect to its nature, so too can a person who does not develop morally be said to have failed.

The life cultivated in virtue will develop and mature morally. It is for this reason that the virtues must guide action in Stoic doctrine. The most important Stoic virtues are courage, temperance, prudence, and justice. For the Stoics, a life without these virtues is bestial, unbecoming of humanity. Further, these virtues are interdependent. One may be charitable in giving away a house to a friend, but that charity is not a virtue if the house given was stolen from someone else. Charity without justice, then, is in no way honorable. A fully realized human life is governed by virtue in its proper signification, as a well bound web worthy of the name wisdom.

I have in this book collected hundreds of quotes from various Stoic authors. The aim of this collection is to create a general resource or well of wisdom from which the reader can draw for their day-to-day trials. But alone these passages do not give a full picture of the Stoic project. One must fully account for, own up to, their nature as a creature predisposed toward virtue. This for the Stoics means consistent practice and self-reflection. It is not enough to, for example, observe what one can and cannot control when the impetus is disturbing or upsetting, but also when the impetus is self-affirming. It is not enough to say merely that an insult received from another person does not reflect one's own character, but also that a complement is so divorced.

This book is divide into four sections, each representing a season of the year. Besides finding this format aesthetically interesting, the organization of the themes is meant to carry a seasonal flare, with each set matching problems and attitudes often associated with the various seasons. Though the book itself starts in the winter theme, the reader is encouraged to skip around and find the theme that best suits her needs. By the end, it is my hope that she will come to understand Epictetus when he says,

"It has been ordained that there be summer and winter, abundance and dearth, virtue and vice, and all such opposites for the harmony of the whole, and (Zeus) has given each of us a body, property, and companions."

I. Winter Woes

a. **Stoicism and Sadness** – Passages concerning sadness, coping, and revitalizing yourself.

"Show me someone untroubled with disturbing thoughts about illness, danger, death, exile or loss of reputation. By all the gods, I want to see a Stoic!"

Epictetus, *Discourses*

"What really frightens and dismays us is not external events themselves, but the way in which we think about them. It is not things that disturb us, but our interpretation of their significance."

Epictetus, *Discourses*[37]

When you are disturbed by events and lose your serenity, quickly return to yourself and don't stay upset longer than the experience lasts; for you'll have more mastery over your inner harmony by continually returning to it.

---

37   Epictetus, *Discourses*, II, ibid

Marcus Aurelius, *Meditations*

"Fire tests gold, suffering tests brave men."

Seneca, *Letters From a Stoic*[38]

"Whatever happens, happens such as you are either formed by nature able to bear it, or not able to bear it. If such as you are by nature formed able to bear, bear it and fret not: But if such as you are not naturally able to bear, don't fret; for when it has consumed you, itself will perish. Remember, however, you are by nature formed able to bear whatever it is in the power of your own opinion to make supportable or tolerable, according as you conceive it advantageous, or your duty, to do so."

Marcus Aurelius, *Meditations*

"Be free from grief not through insensibility like the irrational animals, nor through want of thought like the foolish, but like a man of virtue by having reason as the consolation of grief."

Epictetus, Fragment[39]

Enough of this miserable, whining life. Stop monkeying around! Why are you troubled? What's new here? What's so confounding? The one responsible? Take a good look. Or just the

---

38 Seneca, Letters *From a Stoic*, Letter I
39 Epictetus, Fragment

matter itself? Then look at that. There's nothing else to look at. And as far as the gods go, by now you could try being more straightforward and kind. It's the same, whether you've examined these things for a hundred years, or only three.

Marcus Aurelius, *Meditations*

"Unhappy am I because this has happened to me.- Not so, but happy am I, though this has happened to me, because I continue free from pain, neither crushed by the present nor fearing the future."

Marcus Aurelius, *Meditations*

Failure to observe what is in the mind of another has seldom made a man unhappy; but those who do not observe the movements of their own minds must of necessity be unhappy.

Marcus Aurelius, *Meditations*[40]

"So let those people go on weeping and wailing whose self-indulgent minds have been weakened by long prosperity, let them collapse at the threat of the most trivial injuries; but let those who have spent all their years suffering disasters endure the worst afflictions with a brave and resolute staunchness.

---

[40] Marcus Aurelius, *Meditations*, IV, III, ibid, II

Everlasting misfortune does have one blessing, that it ends up by toughening those whom it constantly afflicts."

Seneca, *On Shortness of Life*[41]

"Faced with pain, you will discover the power of endurance. If you are insulted, you will discover patience. In time, you will grow to be confident that there is not a single impression that you will not have the moral means to tolerate."

Epictetus, *Enchiridion*[42]

Yes, keep on degrading yourself, soul. But soon your chance at dignity will be gone. Everyone gets one life. Yours is almost used up, and instead of treating yourself with respect, you have entrusted your own happiness to the souls of others.

Marcus Aurelius, *Meditations*

"Wild animals run from the dangers they actually see, and once they have escaped them worry no more. We however are tormented alike by what is past and what is to come. A number of our blessings do us harm, for memory brings back the agony

---

41 Seneca, *On Shortness of Life*, II
42 Epictetus, *Enchiridion*, X

of fear while foresight brings it on prematurely. No one confines his unhappiness to the present."

Seneca, *Letters From a Stoic*[43]

Either all things proceed from one intelligent source and come together as in one body, and the part ought not to find fault with what is done for the benefit of the whole; or there are only atoms, and nothing else than mixture and dispersion. Why, then, are you disturbed?

Marcus Aurelius, *Meditations*[44]

"Your happiness depends on three things, all of which are within your power: your will, your ideas concerning the events in which you are involved, and the use you make of your ideas."

Epictetus, *Discourses*[45]

"Whenever you want to cheer yourself up, consider the good qualities of your companions, for example, the energy of one, the modesty of another, the generosity of yet another, and some other quality of another; for nothing cheers the heart as much as

---

43   Seneca, *Letters From a Stoic*, Letter I
44   Marcus Aurelius, *Meditations*, V, IX
45   Epictetus, *Discourses*, II

the images of excellence reflected in the character of our companions, all brought before us as fully as possible. Therefore, keep these images ready at hand."

Marcus Aurelius, *Meditations*

"Work, therefore to be able to say to every harsh appearance, 'You are but an appearance, and not absolutely the thing you appear to be.' And then examine it by those rules which you have, and first, and chiefly, by this: whether it concerns the things which are in our own control, or those which are not; and, if it concerns anything not in our control, be prepared to say that it is nothing to you."

Epictetus, *Enchiridion*

"If you suppose any of the things not in our own control to be either good or evil, when you are disappointed of what you wish, or incur what you would avoid, you must necessarily find fault with and blame the authors. For every animal is naturally formed to fly and abhor things that appear hurtful, and the causes of them; and to pursue and admire those which appear beneficial, and the causes of them. It is impractical, then, that one who supposes himself to be hurt should be happy about the person who, he thinks, hurts him, just as it is impossible to be happy about the hurt itself."

Epictetus, *Enchiridion*[46]

"So long, in fact, as you remain in ignorance of what to aim at and what to avoid, what is essential and what is superfluous, what is upright or honorable conduct and what is not, it will not be traveling but drifting. All this hurrying from place to place won't bring you any relief, for you're traveling in the company of your own emotions, followed by your troubles all the way."

Seneca, *Letters From a Stoic*[47]

"The true man is revealed in difficult times. So when trouble comes, think of yourself as a wrestler whom God, like a trainer, has paired with a tough young buck. For what purpose? To turn you into Olympic-class material. But this is going to take some sweat to accomplish."

Epictetus, *Discourses*

"Remember from now on whenever something tends to make you unhappy, draw on this principle: 'This is no misfortune; but bearing with it bravely is a blessing.'"

---

[46] Epictetus, *Enchiridion*, I, XXXI
[47] Seneca, *Letters From a Stoic*, Letter I

Epictetus, *Discourses*[48]

b. **Deprecation and Anger** – How to handle changing moods, especially the strongest one.

"Remember, it is not enough to be hit or insulted to be harmed, you must believe that you are being harmed. If someone succeeds in provoking you, realize that your mind is complicit in the provocation. Which is why it is essential that we not respond impulsively to impressions; take a moment before reacting, and you will find it easier to maintain control."

Epictetus, *Discourses*[49]

"Anger cannot be dishonest."

Marcus Aurelius, *Meditations*

"A physician is not angry at the intemperance of a mad patient; nor does he take it ill to be railed at by a man in a fever. Just so should a wise man treat all mankind, as a physician does his patient; and looking upon them only as sick and extravagant."

Seneca, *Letters From a Stoic*[50]

---

[48] Epictetus, *Discourses*, II, IV
[49] Epictetus, *Discourses*, I
[50] Seneca, *Letters From a Stoic*, Letter II

It is a proper work of a man to be benevolent to his own kind, to despise the movements of the senses, to form a just judgment of plausible appearances, and to take a survey of the nature of the universe and of the things that happen in it.

Marcus Aurelius, *Meditations*

"Men decide far more problems by hate, love, lust, rage, sorrow, joy, hope, fear, illusion, or some other inward emotion than by reality, authority, any legal standard, judicial precedent, or statute."

Cicero, *De Oratore*[51]

Consider what men are when they are eating, sleeping, coupling, evacuating, and so forth. Then what kind of men they are when they are imperious and arrogant, or angry and scolding from their elevated place.

Marcus Aurelius, *Meditations*

"An innocent man, if accused, can be acquitted; a guilty man, unless accused, cannot be condemned. It is, however, more advantageous to absolve an innocent than not to prosecute a guilty man."

---

51   Cicero, *De Oratore*

Cicero, *On Anger*[52]

"As for others whose lives are not so ordered, he reminds himself constantly of the characters they exhibit daily and nightly at home and abroad, and of the sort of society they frequent; and the approval of such men, who do not even stand well in their own eyes, has no value for him."

Marcus Aurelius, *Meditations*[53]

"As fire when thrown into water is cooled down and put out, so also a false accusation when brought against a man of the purest and holiest character, boils over and is at once dissipated, and vanishes and threats of heaven and sea, himself standing unmoved."

Cicero, *On Anger*[54]

"Nothing is burdensome if taken lightly, and nothing need arouse one's irritation so long as one doesn't make it bigger than it is by getting irritated."

Seneca, *Letters From a Stoic*

---

[52] Cicero, *On Anger*, II
[53] Marcus Aurelius, *Meditations*, II, VI, ibid, III
[54] Cicero, *On Anger*, I

This, then, is consistent with the character of a reflecting man, to be neither careless nor impatient nor contemptuous with respect to death, but to wait for it as one of the operations of nature.

Marcus Aurelius, *Meditations*

'My brother shouldn't have treated me in this way.' Indeed he shouldn't, but it's for him to see to that. For my part, however he treats me, I should conduct myself towards him as I ought. For that is my business, and the rest is not my concern. In this no one can hinder me, while everything else is subject to hindrance."

Epictetus, *Discourses*[55]

Consider that you also do many things wrong, and that you are a man like others; and even if you do abstain from certain faults, still you have the disposition to commit them, though either through cowardice, or concern about reputation, or some such mean motive, you abstain from such faults.

Marcus Aurelius, *Meditations*[56]

"Treat unenlightened souls with sympathy and indulgence, remembering that they are ignorant or mistaken about what's

---

55   Epictetus, *Discourses*, III, II
56   Marcus Aurelius, *Meditations*, IX, IV

most important. Never be harsh, remember Plato's dictum: 'Every soul is deprived of the truth against its will.'"

Epictetus, *Discourses*

"If you really want to escape the things that harass you, what you're needing is not to be in a different place but to be a different person."

Seneca, *Letters From a Stoic*[57]

Whatever any one does or says, I must be good, just as if the emerald (or the gold or the purple) were always saying "Whatever any one does or says, I must be emerald and keep my color."

Marcus Aurelius, *Meditations*

If you don't want to be cantankerous, don't feed your temper, or multiply incidents of anger. Suppress the first impulse to be angry, then begin to count the days on which you don't get mad.

---

57 Seneca, *Letters From a Stoic,* Letter II, ibid

Marcus Aurelius, *Meditations*

"He did not say, 'Define me envy', and then, when the man defined it, 'You define it ill, for the terms of the definition do not correspond to the subject defined.' Such phrases are technical and therefore tiresome to the lay mind, and hard to follow, yet you and I cannot get away from them. We are quite unable to rouse the ordinary man's attention in a way which will enable him to follow his own impressions and so arrive at admitting or rejecting this or that. And therefore those of us who are at all cautious naturally give the subject up, when we become aware of this incapacity; while the mass of men, who venture at random into this sort of enterprise, muddle others and get muddled themselves, and end by abusing their opponents and getting abused in return, and so leave the field. But the first quality of all in Socrates, and the most characteristic, was that he never lost his temper in argument, never uttered anything abusive, never anything insolent, but bore with abuse from others and quieted strife."

Epictetus, *Enchiridion*[58]

Who wants to live with delusion and prejudice, being unjust, undisciplined, mean and ungrateful? 'No one.' No bad person, then, lives the way he wants, and no bad man is free.

---

58   Epictetus, *Enchiridion*

Marcus Aurelius, *Meditations*

"For what does the man who accepts insult do that is wrong? It is the doer of wrong who puts themselves to shame-the sensible man wouldn't go to the law, since he wouldn't even consider that he had been insulted! Besides, to be annoyed or angered about such things would be petty-instead easily and silently bear what has happened, since this is appropriate for those whose purpose is to be noble-minded."

Musonius Rufus, *How To Live*[59]

"If any man despises me, that is his problem. My only concern is not doing or saying anything deserving of contempt."

Marcus Aurelius, *Meditations*[60]

"....nothing cruel is in fact beneficial; for cruelty is extremely hostile to the nature of man, which we ought to follow."

Cicero, *On Anger*[61]

With what are you discontented? With the badness of men? Recall to your mind this conclusion, that rational animals exist

---

[59] Musonius Rufus, *How To Live*
[60] Marcus Aurelius, *Meditations*, VII, II, III
[61] Cicero, *On Anger*

for one another, and that to endure is a part of justice, and that men do wrong involuntarily.

Marcus Aurelius, *Meditations*

"When you wake up in the morning, tell yourself: the people I deal with today will be meddling, ungrateful, arrogant, dishonest, jealous and surly. They are like this because they can't tell good from evil. But I have seen the beauty of good, and the ugliness of evil, and have recognized that the wrongdoer has a nature related to my own - not of the same blood and birth, but the same mind, and possessing a share of the divine. And so none of them can hurt me. No one can implicate me in ugliness. Nor can I feel angry at my relative, or hate him. We were born to work together like feet, hands and eyes, like the two rows of teeth, upper and lower. To obstruct each other is unnatural. To feel anger at someone, to turn your back on him: these are unnatural."

Marcus Aurelius, *Meditations*

"To accuse others for one's own misfortune is a sign of want of education. To accuse oneself shows that one's education has begun. To accuse neither oneself nor others shows that one's education is complete."

Epictetus, *Enchiridion*[62]

"How much more grievous are the consequences of anger than the causes of it."

Marcus Aurelius, *Meditations*

"Men seek retreats for themselves, houses in the country, seashores, and mountains; and thou too art wont to desire such things very much. But this is altogether a mark of the most common sort of men, for it is in thy power whenever thou shalt choose to retire into thyself. For nowhere either with more quiet or more freedom from trouble does a man retire than into his own soul, particularly when he has within him such thoughts that by looking into them he is immediately in perfect tranquility; and I affirm that tranquility is nothing else than the good ordering of the mind."

Marcus Aurelius, *Meditations*[63]

"What, for instance, does it mean to be insulted? Stand by a rock and insult it, and what have you accomplished? If someone responds to insult like a rock, what has the abuser gained with

---

62   Epictetus, *Enchiridion*, V
63   Marcus Aurelius, *Meditations*, IV, II, I, IV

his invective? If, however, he has his victim's weakness to exploit, then his efforts are worth his while."

Epictetus, *Of Human Freedom*[64]

When a guide meets up with someone who is lost, ordinarily his reaction is to direct him on the right path, not mock or malign him, then turn on his heel and walk away. As for you, lead someone to the truth and you will find that he can follow. But as long as you don't point it out to him, don't make fun of him; be aware of what you need to work on instead.

Marcus Aurelius, *Meditations*

"Some things are in our control and others not. Things in our control are opinion, pursuit, desire, aversion, and, in a word, whatever are our own actions. Things not in our control are body, property, reputation, command, and, in one word, whatever are not our actions. The things in our control are by nature free, unrestrained, unhindered; but those not in our control are weak, slavish, restrained, belonging to others. Remember, then, that if you suppose that things which are slavish by nature are also free, and that what belongs to others is your own, then you will be hindered. You will lament, you will

---

64   Epictetus, *Of Human Freedom*

be disturbed, and you will find fault both with gods and men. But if you suppose that only to be your own which is your own, and what belongs to others such as it really is, then no one will ever compel you or restrain you. Further, you will find fault with no one or accuse no one. You will do nothing against your will. No one will hurt you, you will have no enemies, and you not be harmed."

Epictetus, *Enchiridion*[65]

"The best revenge is to be unlike him who performed the injury."

Marcus Aurelius, *Meditations*

"You always own the option of having no opinion. There is never any need to get worked up or to trouble your soul about things you can't control. These things are not asking to be judged by you. Leave them alone."

Marcus Aurelius, *Meditations*

"Regain your senses, call yourself back, and once again wake up. Now that you realize that only dreams were troubling you, view this 'reality' as you view your dreams."

---

[65] Epictetus, *Enchiridion*, I

Marcus Aurelius, *Meditations*[66]

"When people injure you, ask yourself what good or harm they thought would come of it. If you understand that, you'll feel sympathy rather than outrage or anger. Your sense of good and evil may be the same as theirs, or near it, in which case you have to excuse them. Or your sense of good and evil may differ from theirs. In which case they're misguided and deserve your compassion. Is that so hard?"

Marcus Aurelius, *Meditations*

c. **Motivation** – Stoic tips for staying active.

You have leisure or ability to check arrogance: you have leisure to be superior to pleasure and pain: you have leisure to be superior to love of fame, and not to be vexed at stupid and ungrateful people, nay even to care for them.

Marcus Aurelius, *Meditations*

"Your greatest difficulty is with yourself; for you are your own stumbling-block. You do not know what you want. You are better at approving the right course than at following it out. You see where the true happiness lies, but you have not the courage to attain it."

---

66   Marcus Aurelius, *Meditations*, II, I, ibid, V, IV

Seneca, *Letters From a Stoic*[67]

Nothing important comes into being overnight; even grapes or figs need time to ripen. If you say that you want a fig now, I will tell you to be patient. First, you must allow the tree to flower, then put forth fruit; then you have to wait until the fruit is ripe. So if the fruit of a fig tree is not brought to maturity instantly or in an hour, how do you expect the human mind to come to fruition, so quickly and easily?

Epictetus, *Discourses*

"It is not reasonings that are wanted now,' he says, 'for there are books stuffed full of stoical reasonings. What is wanted, then? The man who shall apply them; whose actions may bear testimony to his doctrines. Assume this character for me, that we may no longer make use in the schools of the examples of the ancients, but may have some examples of our own."

Epictetus, *Discourses*[68]

"In your actions, don't procrastinate. In your conversations, don't confuse In your thoughts, don't wander. In your soul, don't be passive or aggressive. In your life, don't be all about business."

---

67 Seneca, *Letters From a Stoic*, Letter 21
68 Epictetus, *Discourses*, II, I

Marcus Aurelius, *Meditations*[69]

"When you're called upon to speak, then speak, but never about banalities like gladiators, horses, sports, food and drink – common-place stuff. Above all don't gossip about people, praising, blaming or comparing them."

Marcus Aurelius, *Meditations*

"Continue to act thus, my dear Lucilius – set yourself free for your own sake; gather and save your time, which till lately has been forced from you, or filched away, or has merely slipped from your hands. Make yourself believe the truth of my words, – that certain moments are torn from us, that some are gently removed, and that others glide beyond our reach. The most disgraceful kind of loss, however, is that due to carelessness. Furthermore, if you will pay close heed to the problem, you will find that the largest portion of our life passes while we are doing ill, a goodly share while we are doing nothing, and the whole while we are doing that which is not to the purpose. What man can you show me who places any value on his time, who reckons the worth of each day, who understands that he is dying daily? For we are mistaken when we look forward to death; the major portion of death has already passed. Whatever years be behind us are in death's hands."

---

[69] Marcus Aurelius, *Meditations*, VIII, IV, II

Seneca, *Letters From a Stoic*[70]

"Set yourself in motion, if it is in your power, and do not look about you to see if anyone will observe it; nor yet expect Plato's Republic: but be content if the smallest thing goes on well, and consider such an event to be no small matter.'

Marcus Aurelius, *Meditations*[71]

"What then, is it not possible to be free from faults? It is not possible; but this is possible: to direct your efforts incessantly to being faultless. For we must be content if by never remitting this attention we shall escape at least a few errors. When you have said "Tomorrow I will begin to attend," you must be told that you are saying this: "Today I will be shameless, disregardful of time and place, mean;it will be in the power of others to give me pain, today I will be passionate and envious.

See how many evil things you are permitting yourself to do. If it is good to use attention tomorrow, how much better is it to do so today? If tomorrow it is in your interest to attend, much more is it today, that you may be able to do so tomorrow also, and may not defer it again to the third day."

---

70 Seneca, *Letters From a Stoic*, Letter 10, Letter 13
71 Marcus Aurelius, *Meditations*, XII, III

Epictetus, *Discourses*

"Nothing important comes into being overnight; even grapes and figs need time to ripen. If you say that you want a fig now, I will tell you to be patient. First, you must allow the tree to flower, then put forth fruit; then you have to wait until the fruit is ripe. So if the fruit of a fig tree is not brought to maturity instantly or in an hour, how do you expect the human mind to come to fruition, so quickly and easily?"

Epictetus, *Discourses* [72]

"It is in your power to live here. But if men do not permit you, then get away out of life, as if you were suffering no harm. The house is smoky, and I quit it. Why do you think that this is any trouble? But so long as nothing of the kind drives me out, I remain, am free, and no man shall hinder me from doing what I choose; and I choose to do what is according to the nature of the rational and social animal."

Marcus Aurelius, *Meditations*

"I never spend a day in idleness; I appropriate even a part of the night for study. I do not allow time for sleep but yield to it when

---

[72] Epictetus, *Discourses*, IV

I must, and when my eyes are wearied with waking and ready to fall shut, I keep them at their task."

Seneca, *Letters From a Stoic*

"And so there is no reason for you to think that any man has lived long because he has grey hairs or wrinkles, he has not lived long – he has existed long. For what if you should think that man had had a long voyage who had been caught by a fierce storm as soon as he left harbour, and, swept hither and thither by a succession of winds that raged from different quarters, had been driven in a circle around the same course? Not much voyaging did he have, but much tossing about."

Seneca, *On Shortness of Life*[73]

"At dawn, when you have trouble getting out of bed, tell yourself, "I have to go to work - as a human being. What do I have to complain of, if I'm going to do what I was born for - the things I was brought into the world to do? Or is this what I was created for? To huddle under the blankets and stay warm?"

---

[73] Seneca, *On Shortness of Life*

Marcus Aurelius, *Meditations*[74]

"It is not that we have a short time to live, but that we waste a lot of it. Life is long enough, and a sufficiently generous amount has been given to us for the highest achievements if it were all well invested. But when it is wasted in heedless luxury and spent on no good activity, we are forced at last by death's final constraint to realize that it has passed away before we knew it was passing. So it is: we are not given a short life but we make it short, and we are not ill-supplied but wasteful of it... Life is long if you know how to use it."

Seneca, *Letters From a Stoic*[75]

"Most of what passes for legitimate entertainment is inferior or foolish and only caters to or exploits people's weaknesses. Avoid being one of the mob who indulges in such pastimes. Your life is too short and you have important things to do. Be discriminating about what images and ideas you permit into your mind. If you yourself don't choose what thoughts and images you expose yourself to, someone else will, and their motives may not be the highest. It is the easiest thing in the world to slide imperceptibly into vulgarity. But there's no need

---

[74] Marcus Aurelius, *Meditations*, V, I
[75] Seneca, *Letters From a Stoic*, Letter 12

for that to happen if you determine not to waste your time and attention on mindless pap."

Epictetus, *Discourses*[76]

"Concentrate every minute like a Roman— like a man— on doing what's in front of you with precise and genuine seriousness, tenderly, willingly, with justice. And on freeing yourself from all other distractions. Yes, you can— if you do everything as if it were the last thing you were doing in your life, and stop being aimless, stop letting your emotions override what your mind tells you, stop being hypocritical, self-centered , irritable. You see how few things you have to do to live a satisfying and reverent life? If you can manage this, that's all even the gods can ask of you."

Marcus Aurelius, *Meditations*

"The chief task in life is simply this: to identify and separate matters so that I can say clearly to myself which are externals not under my control, and which have to do with the choices I actually control. Where then do I look for good and evil? Not to uncontrollable externals, but within myself to the choices that are my own..."

---

76   Epictetus, *Discourses*, IV

Epictetus, *Discourses*[77]

"If anyone says that the best life of all is to sail the sea, and then adds that I must not sail upon a sea where shipwrecks are a common occurrence and there are often sudden storms that sweep the helmsman in an adverse direction, I conclude that this man, although he lauds navigation, really forbids me to launch my ship."

Seneca, *On The Shortness of Life*

"Putting things off is the biggest waste of life: it snatches away each day as it comes, and denies us the present by promising the future. The greatest obstacle to living is expectancy, which hangs upon tomorrow, and loses today. You are arranging what lies in Fortune's control, and abandoning what lies in yours. What are you looking at? To what goal are you straining? The whole future lies in uncertainty: live immediately."

Seneca, *On The Shortness of Life*[78]

"Look well into thyself; there is a source of strength which will always spring up if thou wilt always look."

---

77 Epictetus, *Discourses*, II
78 Seneca, *On The Shortness of Life*

Marcus Aurelius, *Meditations*[79]

"How long are you going to wait before you demand the best for yourself and in no instance bypass the discrimination of reason? You have been given the principles that you ought to endorse, and you have endorsed them. What kind of teacher, then, are you still waiting for in order to refer your self-improvement to him? You are no longer a boy, but a full-grown man. If you are careless and lazy now and keep putting things off and always deferring the day after which you will attend to yourself, you will not notice that you are making no progress, but you will live and die as someone quite ordinary."

Epictetus, *Enchiridion*[80]

"Stop wandering about! You aren't likely to read your own notebooks, or ancient histories, or the anthologies you've collected to enjoy in your old age. Get busy with life's purpose, toss aside empty hopes, get active in your own rescue-if you care for yourself at all-and do it while you can."

---

[79] Marcus Aurelius, *Meditations*, I, ibid
[80] Epictetus, *Enchiridion*, 22

Marcus Aurelius, *Meditations*

"As the sun does not wait for prayers and incantations to be induced to rise, but immediately shines and is saluted by all, so do you also not wait for clapping of hands and shouts of praise to be induced to do good, but be a doer of good voluntarily and you will be beloved as much as the sun."

Epictetus, *Discourses*

"A noble man compares and estimates himself by an idea which is higher than himself; and a mean man, by one lower than himself. The one produces aspiration; the other ambition, which is the way in which a vulgar man aspires."

Marcus Aurelius, *Meditations*[81]

"You will do the greatest services to the state, if you shall raise not the roofs of the houses, but the souls of the citizens: for it is better that great souls should dwell in small houses than for mean slaves to lurk in great houses."

---

81   Marcus Aurelius, *Meditations*, V

Epictetus, *Enchiridion*[82]

"What would have become of Hercules do you think if there had been no lion, hydra, stag or boar - and no savage criminals to rid the world of? What would he have done in the absence of such challenges?

Obviously he would have just rolled over in bed and gone back to sleep. So by snoring his life away in luxury and comfort he never would have developed into the mighty Hercules.

And even if he had, what good would it have done him? What would have been the use of those arms, that physique, and that noble soul, without crises or conditions to stir into him action?"

Epictetus, *Discourses*[83]

"Can anything be more idiotic than certain people who boast of their foresight? They keep themselves officiously preoccupied in order to improve their lives; they spend their lives in organizing their lives. They direct their purposes with an eye to a distant future. But putting things off is the biggest waste of life: it snatches away each day as it comes, and denies us the present by promising the future. The greatest obstacle to living is expectancy, which hangs upon tomorrow and loses today. You are arranging what lies in Fortune's control, and abandoning

---

82   Epictetus, *Enchiridion*
83   Epictetus, *Discourses*, II, ibid

what lies in yours. What are you looking at? To what goal are you straining?"

Seneca, *Letters From a Stoic*[84]

"If you have an earnest desire towards philosophy, prepare yourself from the very first to have the multitude laugh and sneer, and say, "He is returned to us a philosopher all at once; "and "Whence this supercilious look?" Now, for your part, do not have a supercilious look indeed; but keep steadily to those things which appear best to you, as one appointed by God to this particular station. For remember that, if you are persistent, those very persons who at first ridiculed will afterwards admire you. But if you are conquered by them, you will incur a double ridicule."

Epictetus, *Enchiridion*[85]

d. **Fear, Regret and New Beginnings** – Overcoming discrepancies between how you saw yourself last year and how you see yourself now.

Don't waste the rest of your time here worrying about other people – unless it affects the common good. It will keep you

---

84 Seneca, *Letters From a Stoic,* **Letter 20**
85 Epictetus, *Enchiridion*

from doing anything useful. You'll be too preoccupied with what so-and-so is doing, and why, and what they're saying, and what they're thinking, and what they're up to, and all the other things that throw you off and keep you from focusing on your own mind.

Marcus Aurelius, *Meditations*

"Limiting one's desires actually helps to cure one of fear. 'Cease to hope ... and you will cease to fear.' ... Widely different [as fear and hope] are, the two of them march in unison like a prisoner and the escort he is handcuffed to. Fear keeps pace with hope ... both belong to a mind in suspense, to a mind in a state of anxiety through looking into the future. Both are mainly due to projecting our thoughts far ahead of us instead of adapting ourselves to the present."

Seneca, *Letters From a Stoic*[86]

"Today I escaped anxiety. Or no, I discarded it, because it was within me, in my own perceptions — not outside."

---

[86] Seneca, *Letters From a Stoic*, Letter 3

Marcus Aurelius, *Meditations*[87]

"Fear is the cause -not exile. To many people, even to most, despite living safely in their home city, fear of what seem to them the dire consequences of free speech is present. The courageous, in exile or at home, is fearless in the face of all such threats; for that reason they've the courage to say what they think equally at home or in exile."

Musonius Rufus, *How To Live*[88]

"When force of circumstance upsets your equanimity, lose no time in recovering your self-control, and do not remain out of tune longer than you can help. Habitual recurrence to the harmony will increase your mastery of it."

Marcus Aurelius, Meditations

"But is life really worth so much? Let us examine this; it's a different inquiry. We will offer no solace for so desolate a prison house; we will encourage no one to endure the over lordship of butchers. We shall rather show that in every kind of slavery, the road of freedom lies open. I will say to the man to whom it befell to have a king shoot arrows at his dear ones, and to him whose

---

87   Marcus Aurelius, *Meditations*, V, II, V
88   Musonius Rufus, *How To Live*

master makes fathers banquet on their sons' guts: 'What are you groaning for, fool?... Everywhere you look you find an end to your sufferings. You see that steep drop- off? It leads down to freedom. You see that ocean, that river, that well? Freedom lies at its bottom. You see that short, shriveled, bare tree? Freedom hangs from it.... You ask, what is the path to freedom? Any vein in your body."

Seneca, *Letters From a Stoic*

"So what oppresses and scares us? It is our own thoughts, obviously, What overwhelms people when they are about to leaves friends, family, old haunts and their accustomed way of life? Thoughts."

Epictetus, *Discourses*[89]

"Live a good life. If there are gods and they are just, then they will not care how devout you have been, but will welcome you based on the virtues you have lived by. If there are gods, but unjust, then you should not want to worship them. If there are no gods, then you will be gone, but will have lived a noble life that will live on in the memories of your loved ones."

---

[89] Epictetus, *Discourses*, II

Marcus Aurelius, *Meditations*[90]

"The trip doesn't exist that can set you beyond the reach of cravings, fits of temper, or fears ... so long as you carry the sources of your troubles about with you, those troubles will continue to harass and plague you wherever you wander on land or on sea. Does it surprise you that running away doesn't do you any good? The things you're running away from are with you all the time."

Seneca, *Letters From a Stoic*[91]

"As for us, we behave like a herd of deer. When they flee from the huntsman's feathers in affright, which way do they turn? What haven of safety do they make for? Why, they rush upon the nets! And thus they perish by confounding what they should fear with that wherein no danger lies. . . . Not death or pain is to be feared, but the fear of death or pain. Well said the poet therefore: —

Death has no terror; only a Death of shame!"

---

[90] Marcus Aurelius, *Meditations*, III, I
[91] Seneca, *Letters From a Stoic*, Letter 24

Epictetus, *Fragments*[92]

"Do not waste what remains of your life in speculating about your neighbors, unless with a view to some mutual benefit. To wonder what so-and-so is doing and why, or what he is saying, or thinking, or scheming—in a word, anything that distracts you from fidelity to the ruler within you—means a loss of opportunity for some other task."

Marcus Aurelius, *Meditations*

"The gods do not exists, and even if they exist they do not trouble themselves about people, and we have nothing in common with them. The piety and devotion to the gods that the majority of people invoke is a lie devised by swindlers and con men and, if you can believe it, by legislators, to keep criminals in line by putting the fear of God into them."

Epictetus, *Discourses*

"Do not disturb yourself by picturing your life as a whole; do not assemble in your mind the many and varied troubles which have come to you in the past and will come again in the future, but ask yourself with regard to every present difficulty: 'What is there in this that is unbearable and beyond endurance?' You

---

92   Epictetus, Fragment

would be ashamed to confess it! And then remind yourself that it is not the future or what has passed that afflicts you, but always the present, and the power of this is much diminished if you take it in isolation and call your mind to task if it thinks that it cannot stand up to it when taken on its own."

Marcus Aurelius, *Meditations*[93]

"With every accident, ask yourself what abilities you have for making a proper use of it. If you see an attractive person, you will find that self-restraint is the ability you have against your desire. If you are in pain, you will find fortitude. If you hear unpleasant language, you will find patience. And thus habituated, the appearances of things will not hurry you away along with them."

Epictetus, *Enchiridion* [94]

"Two elements must therefore be rooted out once for all, – the fear of future suffering, and the recollection of past suffering; since the latter no longer concerns me, and the former concerns me not yet."

---

93 Marcus Aurelius, *Meditations*, II
94 Epictetus, *Enchiridion*

Seneca, *Letters From a Stoic*[95]

II. Spring in Bloom

a. **Relinquishing the Past** – Passages on forgiveness.

"Philosophy does not promise to secure anything external for man, otherwise it would be admitting something that lies beyond its proper subject-matter. For as the material of the carpenter is wood, and that of statuary bronze, so the subject-matter of the art of living is each person's own life."

Epictetus, *Discourses*[96]

"You have the power to strip away many superfluous troubles located wholly in your judgment, and to possess a large room for yourself embracing in thought the whole cosmos, to consider everlasting time, to think of the rapid change in the parts of each thing, of how short it is from birth until dissolution, and how the void before birth and that after dissolution are equally infinite."

Marcus Aurelius, *Meditations*

"To see a man fearless in dangers, untainted with lusts, happy in adversity, composed in a tumult, and laughing at all those things which are generally either coveted or feared, all men must acknowledge that this can be from nothing else but a beam of divinity that influences a mortal body."

---

96   Epictetus, *Discourses*, I, III

Seneca, *Letters From a Stoic*

"To admonish is better than to reproach for admonition is mild and friendly, but reproach is harsh and insulting; and admonition corrects those who are doing wrong, but reproach only convicts them."

Epictetus, Enchiridion[97]

"Whenever you are about to find fault with someone, ask yourself the following question: What fault of mine most nearly resembles the one I am about to criticize?"

Marcus Aurelius, *Meditations*[98]

"No man has ever been so far advanced by Fortune that she did not threaten him as greatly as she had previously indulged him. Do not trust her seeming calm; in a moment the sea is moved to its depths. The very day the ships have made a brave show in the games, they are engulfed."

---

97 Epictetus, *Enchiridion*
98 Marcus Aurelius, *Meditations*, V, VII

Seneca, *Letters From a Stoic*[99]

"Does anyone bathe hastily? Do not say that they do it ill, but hastily. Does anyone drink much wine? Do not say that they do ill, but that they drink a great deal. For unless you perfectly understand their motives, how should you know if they act ill? Thus you will not risk yielding to any appearances except those you fully comprehend."

Epictetus, *Enchiridion*[100]

It is just charming how people boast about qualities beyond their control. For instance, 'I am better than you because I have many estates, while you are practically starving'; or, 'I'm a consul,' 'I'm a governor,' or 'I have fine curly hair.'

Marcus Aurelius, *Meditations*

"To help us to cheerfully endure those hardships which we may expect to suffer because of virtue and goodness, it is useful to recall what hardships people will endure for immoral reasons. Consider what lustful lovers undergo for the sake of evil desires- and how much exertion others expend for the sake of profit-how much suffering pursuing fame - bear in mind that they all submit

---

99   Seneca, *Letters From a Stoic*, Letter 57
100   Epictetus, *Enchiridion*, X

to all kinds of toil and hardship voluntarily. It's monstrous that they endure such things for no honourable reward, yet for the sake of the good (not only the avoidance of evil that wrecks our lives-also the gain of virtue) we're not ready to bear the slightest hardship."

Musonius Rufus, *On How To Live*[101]

"You should be especially careful when associating with one of your former friends or acquaintances not to sink to their level; otherwise you will lose yourself. If you are troubled by the idea that 'He'll think I'm boring and won't treat me the way he used to,' remember that everything comes at a price. It isn't possible to change your behavior and still be the same person you were before."

Epictetus, *Discourses*

b. **Self-Image** – Stoic advice for self-perception, focusing on control (or lack thereof) of one's appetites and health.

"You know yourself what you are worth in your own eyes; and at what price you will sell yourself. For men sell themselves at various prices. This is why, when Florus was deliberating

---

[101] Musonius Rufus, *On How To Live*

whether he should appear at Nero's shows, taking part in the performance himself, Agrippinus replied, 'Appear by all means.' And when Florus inquired, 'But why do not you appear?' he answered, 'Because I do not even consider the question.' For the man who has once stooped to consider such questions, and to reckon up the value of external things, is not far from forgetting what manner of man he is."

Epictetus, *Discourses*[102]

"Because your own strength is unequal to the task, do not assume that it is beyond the powers of man; but if anything is within the powers and province of man, believe that it is within your own compass also."

Marcus Aurelius, *Meditations*[103]

"Why be concerned about others, come to that, when you've outdone your own self? Set yourself a limit which you couldn't even exceed if you wanted to, and say good-bye at last to those deceptive prizes more precious to those who hope for them than to those who have won them. If there were anything substantial in them they would sooner or later bring a sense of

---

[102] Epictetus, Discourses, IV, II
[103] Marcus Aurelius, *Meditations*, III

fullness; as it is they simply aggravate the thirst of those who swallow them."

Seneca, *Letters From a Stoic*[104]

"You ought to realize, you take up very little space in the world as a whole – your body, that is; in reason, however, you yield to no one, not even to the gods, because reason is not measured in size but sense. So why not care for that side of you, where you and the gods are equals?"

Marcus Aurelius, *Meditations*

"I believe that no characteristic is so distinctively human as the sense of indebtedness we feel, not necessarily for a favor received, but even for the slightest evidence of kindness; and there is nothing so boorish, savage, inhuman as to appear to be overwhelmed by a favor, let alone unworthy of it."

Cicero, *On Old Age*

"When you have done a good act and another has received it, why do you look for a third thing besides these, as fools do, either to have the reputation of having done a good act or to obtain a return? If money is your only standard, then consider

---

[104] Seneca, *Letters From a Stoic*, Letter 33

that, by your lights, someone who loses their nose does not suffer any harm."

Marcus Aurelius, *Meditations*

We are motivated by a keen desire for praise, and the better a man is the more he is inspired by glory. The very philosophers themselves, even in those books which they write in contempt of glory, inscribe their names.

Cicero, *On Old Age*[105]

"Never depend on the admiration of others. There is no strength in it. Personal merit cannot be derived from an external source. It is not to be found in your personal associations, nor can it be found in the regard of other people. It is a fact of life that other people, even people who love you, will not necessarily agree with your ideas, understand you, or share your enthusiasms. Grow up! Who cares what other people think about you!"

Epictetus, *Enchiridion*

"How strangely men act. They will not praise those who are living at the same time and living with themselves; but to be themselves praised by posterity, by those whom they have never seen or ever will see, this they set much value on."

---

105   Cicero, *On Old Age*

Marcus Aurelius, *Meditations*

"Do as Socrates did, never replying to the question of where he was from with, 'I am Athenian,' or 'I am from Corinth,' but always, 'I am a citizen of the world.'"

Marcus Aurelius, *Meditations*[106]

"I imagine many people could have achieved wisdom if they had not imagined they had already achieved it, if they had not dissembled about some of their own characteristics and turned a blind eye to others."

Seneca, *Letters From a Stoic*[107]

"So you know how things stand. Now forget what they think of you. Be satisfied if you can live the rest of your life, however short, as your nature demands. Focus on that, and don't let anything distract you. You've wandered all over and finally realized that you never found what you were after: how to live. Not in syllogisms, not in money, or fame, or self-indulgence. Nowhere."

---

106   Marcus Aurelius, *Meditations*, II, IV, ibid
107   Seneca, *Letters From a Stoic*, Letter 28

Marcus Aurelius, *Meditations*

"A person's worth is measured by the worth of what he values."

Marcus Aurelius, *Meditations*

"When any person harms you, or speaks badly of you, remember that he acts or speaks from a supposition of its being his duty. Now, it is not possible that he should follow what appears right to you, but what appears so to himself. Therefore, if he judges from a wrong appearance, he is the person hurt, since he too is the person deceived. For if anyone should suppose a true proposition to be false, the proposition is not hurt, but he who is deceived about it. Setting out, then, from these principles, you will meekly bear a person who reviles you, for you will say upon every occasion, "It seemed so to him.""

Epictetus, *Enchiridion*[108]

"The happiness of those who want to be popular depends on others; the happiness of those who seek pleasure fluctuates with moods outside their control; but the happiness of the wise grows out of their own free acts."

---

[108] Epictetus, *Enchiridion*

Marcus Aurelius, *Meditations*[109]

"-Who are those people by whom you wish to be admired? Are they not these whom you are in the habit of saying that they are mad? What then? Do you wish to be admired by the mad?"

Epictetus, *Discourses*

"Never value anything as profitable that compels you to break your promise, to lose your self-respect, to hate any man, to suspect, to curse, to act the hypocrite, to desire anything that needs walls and curtains."

Marcus Aurelius, *Meditations*

"Crows pick out the eyes of the dead, when the dead have no longer need of them; but flatterers mar the soul of the living, and her eyes they blind."

Epictetus, *Discourses*[110]

"In your conversation, don't dwell at excessive length on your own deeds or adventures. Just because you enjoy recounting your exploits doesn't mean that others derive the same pleasure from hearing about them."

---

109 Marcus Aurelius, *Meditations*, IV, ibid, II
110 Epictetus, *Discourses*, II, ibid

Marcus Aurelius, *Meditations*[111]

"And this, too, affords no small occasion for anxieties - if you are bent on assuming a pose and never reveal yourself to anyone frankly, in the fashion of many who live a false life that is all made up for show; for it is torturous to be constantly watching oneself and be fearful of being caught out of our usual role. And we are never free from concern if we think that every time anyone looks at us he is always taking-our measure; for many things happen that strip off our pretense against our will, and, though all this attention to self is successful, yet the life of those who live under a mask cannot be happy and without anxiety. But how much pleasure there is in simplicity that is pure, in itself unadorned, and veils no part of its character! Yet even such a life as this does run some risk of scorn, if everything lies open to everybody; for there are those who disdain whatever has become too familiar. But neither does virtue run any risk of being despised when she is brought close to the eyes, and it is better to be scorned by reason of simplicity than tortured by perpetual pretense."

---

111   Marcus Aurelius, *Meditations*, II

Seneca, *Letters From a Stoic*[112]

"In banquets remember that you entertain two guests, body and soul: and whatever you shall have given to the body you soon eject: but what you shall have given to the soul, you keep always."

Epictetus, *Enchiridion*[113]

"Sickness is a problem for the body, not the mind — unless the mind decides that it is a problem. Lameness, too, is the body's problem, not the mind's. Say this to yourself whatever the circumstance and you will find without fail that the problem pertains to something else, not to you."

Epictetus, *Discourses*

"So what you need is not those more radical remedies which we have now finished with - blocking yourself here, being angry with yourself there, threatening yourself sternly somewhere else - but the final treatment, confidence in yourself and the belief that you are on the right path, and not led astray by the many tracks which cross yours of people who are hopeless."

---

[112] Seneca, *Letters From a Stoic*, Letter 3
[113] Epictetus, *Enchiridion*

Seneca, *Shortness of Life*

"Many people who have progressively lowered their personal standards in an attempt to win social acceptance and life's comforts bitterly resent those of philosophical bent who refuse to compromise their spiritual ideals and who seek to better themselves."

Epictetus, *Discourses*[114]

"If a man has reported to you, that a certain person speaks ill of you, do not make any defense to what has been told you: but reply, The man did not know the rest of my faults, for he would not have mentioned these only."

Epictetus, *Enchiridion*[115]

"He who is discontented with what he has, and with what has been granted to him by fortune, is one who is ignorant of the art of living, but he who bears that in a noble spirit, and makes reasonable use of all that comes from it, deserves to be regarded as a good man."

---

[114] Epictetus, *Discourses*, II
[115] Epictetus, *Enchiridion*, 32

Epictetus, *Discourses*[116]

"If someone is able to show me that what I think or do is not right, I will happily change, for I seek the truth, by which no one was ever truly harmed. It is the person who continues in his self-deception and ignorance who is harmed."

Marcus Aurelius, *Meditations*

"The object of life is not to be on the side of the majority, but to escape finding oneself in the ranks of the insane."

Marcus Aurelius, *Meditations*

"I have often wondered how it is that every man loves himself more than all the rest of men, but yet sets less value on his own opinion of himself than on the opinion of others."

Marcus Aurelius, *Meditations*

"When another blames you or hates you, or people voice similar criticisms, go to their souls, penetrate inside and see what sort of people they are. You will realize that there is no need to be racked with anxiety that they should hold any particular opinion about you."

---

116   Epictetus, *Discourses*, II

Marcus Aurelius, *Meditations*

"Or is it your reputation that's bothering you? But look at how soon we're all forgotten. The abyss of endless time that swallows it all. The emptiness of those applauding hands. The people who praise us; how capricious they are, how arbitrary. And the tiny region it takes place. The whole earth a point in space - and most of it uninhabited."

Marcus Aurelius, *Meditations*[117]

b. **Life and Living Well** – Stoic passages on birth and the promise of the future.

"We ought to do good to others as simply as a horse runs, or a bee makes honey, or a vine bears grapes season after season without thinking of the grapes it has borne."

Marcus Aurelius, *Meditations*

"The love of power or money or luxurious living are not the only things which are guided by popular thinking. We take our cue from people's thinking even in the way we feel pain."

---

117   Marcus Aurelius, *Meditations*, II, IV, I, ibid, II

Marcus Aurelius, *Meditations*

" Our situation is like that at a festival. Sheep and cattle are driven to it to be sold, and most people come either to buy or to sell, while only a few come to look at the spectacle of the festival, to see how it is proceeding and why, and who is organizing it, and for what purpose. So also in this festival of the world. Some people are like sheep and cattle and are interested in nothing but their fodder; for in the case of those of you who are interested in nothing but your property, and land, and slaves, and public posts, all of that is nothing more than fodder. Few indeed are those who attend the fair for love of the spectacle, asking, 'What is the universe, then, and who governs it? No one at all? And yet when a city or household cannot survive for even a very short time without someone to govern it and watch over it, how could it be that such a vast and beautiful structure could be kept so well ordered by mere chance and good luck? So there must be someone governing it. What sort of being is he, and how does he govern it? And we who have been created by him, who are we, and what were we created for? Are we bound together with him in some kind of union and interrelationship, or is that not the case?' Such are the thoughts that are aroused in this small collection of people; and from then on, they devote their leisure to this one thing alone, to finding out about the festival before they have to take their leave. What comes about, then? They become an object of mockery for the crowd, just as the spectators at an ordinary festival are mocked by the traders; and even the sheep and cattle, if they had sufficient intelligence, would laugh at those who attach value to anything other than fodder!"

Epictetus, *Discourses*[118]

"Because what is a human being? Part of a community – the community of gods and men, primarily, and secondarily that of the city we happen to inhabit, which is only a microcosm of the universe in too."

Marcus Aurelius, *Meditations*[119]

"Friendship is nothing else than an accord in all things, human and divine, conjoined with mutual goodwill and affection, and I am inclined to think that, with the exception of wisdom, no better thing has been given to man by the immortal gods"

Cicero, *On Friendship*[120]

"You should, I need hardly say, live in such a way that there is nothing which you could not as easily tell your enemy as keep to yourself."

---

118   Epictetus, *Discourses*, III
119   Marcus Aurelius, *Meditations*, II, IV, XI
120   Cicero, *On Friendship*

Seneca, *Letters from a Stoic*[121]

"He who is afraid of pain will sometimes also be afraid of some of the things that will happen in the world, and even this is impiety. And he who pursues pleasure will not abstain from injustice, and this is plainly impiety."

Marcus Aurelius, *Meditations*

"Just what is the civil law? What neither influence can affect, nor power break, nor money corrupt: were it to be suppressed or even merely ignored or inadequately observed, no one would feel safe about anything, whether his own possessions, the inheritance he expects from his father, or the bequests he makes to his children."

Cicero, *Pro Gallio*[122]

"If, at some point in your life, you should come across anything better than justice, honesty, self-control, courage – than a mind satisfied that is has succeeded in enabling you to act rationally, and satisfied to accept what's beyond its control – if you find anything better than that, embrace it without reservations – it must be an extraordinary thing indeed – and enjoy it to the full."

---

121   Seneca, *Letters From a Stoic*, Letter 31
122   Cicero, *Pro Gallio*

Marcus Aurelius, *Meditations*[123]

Just as the soul fills the body, so God fills the world. Just as the soul bears the body, so God endures the world. Just as the soul sees but is not seen, so God sees but is not seen. Just as the soul feeds the body, so God gives food to the world.

Cicero, *On Old Age*[124]

"Thus Socrates became perfect, improving himself by everything. attending to nothing but reason. And though you are not yet a Socrates, you ought, however, to live as one desirous of becoming a Socrates.

Epictetus, *Discourses*[125]

"There were two vices much blacker and more serious than the rest: lack of persistence and lack of self-control... persist and resist."

Marcus Aurelius, *Meditations*

"For while we are enclosed in these confinements of the body, we perform as a kind of duty the heavy task of necessity; for the

---

[123] Marcus Aurelius, *Meditations*, II, I, VI
[124] Cicero, *On Old Age*
[125] Epictetus, *Discourses*, IV

soul from heaven has been cast down from its dwelling on high and sunk, as it were, into the earth, a place just the opposite to godlike nature and eternity. But I believe that the immortal gods have sown souls in human bodies so there might exist beings to guard the world and after contemplating the order of heaven, might imitate it by their moderation and steadfastness in life."

Cicero, *On Old Age*[126]

"What then can guide a man? One thing and only one, philosophy. But this consists in keeping the daimon within a man free from violence and unharmed, superior to pains and pleasures, doing nothing without a purpose, nor yet falsely and with hypocrisy."

Marcus, Aurelius, *Meditations*

"It is not right that anything of any other kind, such as praise from the many, or power, or enjoyment of pleasure, should come into competition with that which is rationally and politically and practically good."

Marcus Aurelius, *Meditations*[127]

---

126   Cicero, *On Old Age*
127   Marcus Aurelius, *Meditations*, II, III

"Yet if we place the good in right choice, the preservation of our relationships itself becomes a good. And besides, he who gives up certain external things achieves the good through that. 'My father's depriving me of money.' But he isn't causing you any harm. 'My brother is going to get the greater share of the land.' Let him have as much as he wishes. He won't be getting any of your decency, will he, or of your loyalty, or of your brotherly love? For who can disinherit you of possessions such as those? Not even Zeus; nor would he wish to, but rather he has placed all of that in my own power, even as he had it himself, free from hindrance, compulsion, and restraint."

Epictetus, *Discourses*[128]

"Just ask whether they put their self-interest in externals or in moral choice. If it's in externals, you cannot call them friends, any more than you can call them trustworthy, consistent, courageous or free."

Marcus Aurelius, *Meditations*

"My advice is really this: what we hear the philosophers saying and what we find in their writings should be applied in our pursuit of the happy life. We should hunt out the helpful pieces of teaching, and the spirited and noble-minded sayings which

---

[128] Epictetus, *Discourses*

are capable of immediate practical application—not far-fetched or archaic expressions or extravagant metaphors and figures of speech—and learn them so well that words become works. No one to my mind lets humanity down quite so much as those who study philosophy as if it were a sort of commercial skill and then proceed to live in a quite different manner from the way they tell other people to live."

Seneca, *Letters From a Stoic*[129]

"Everything that exists is in a manner the seed of that which will be."

Marcus Aurelius, *Meditations*

"And what else can I do, lame old man that I am, than sing the praise of God? If I were a nightingale, I would perform the work of a nightingale, and if I were a swan, that of a swan. But as it is, I am a rational being, and I must sing the praise of God.

This is my work, and I accomplish it, and I will never abandon my post for as long as it is granted to me to remain in it; and I invite all of you to join me in this same song."

---

[129] Seneca, *Letters From a Stoic*, Letter 11

Epictetus, *Discourses*[130]

"But I must at the very beginning lay down this principle—friendship can only exist between good men."

Cicero, *On Friendship*[131]

Adapt yourself to the things among which your lot has been cast and love sincerely the fellow creatures with whom destiny has ordained that you shall live.

Marcus Aurelius, *Meditations*

"Husband and wife should come together to craft a shared life, procreating children, seeing all things as shared between them-with nothing withheld or private to one another-not even their bodies. The birth of a human being which results from this union is, to be sure, something wonderful-but it isn't yet enough to account for the relationship of husband and wife-since even outside marriage it could result from any other sexual union (just as in the case of animals). So, in marriage there must be, above all, perfect companionship and mutual love - both in sickness, health and under all conditions-it should be with desire for this (and children) that both entered upon marriage."

---

[130] Epictetus, *Discourses*, IV
[131] Cicero, *On Friendship*

Musonius Rufus, *How To Live*

"Life will follow the path it started upon, and will neither reverse nor check its course; it will make no noise, it will not remind you of its swiftness. Silent it will glide on; it will not prolong itself at the command of a king, or at the applause of the populace. Just as it was started on its first day, so it will run; nowhere will it turn aside, nowhere will it delay."

Seneca, *On Shortness of Life*

"Whatever is in any way beautiful hath its source of beauty in itself, and is complete in itself; praise forms no part of it. So it is none the worse nor the better for being praised."

Marcus Aurelius, *Meditations*[132]

"Suppose I should say to a wrestler, 'Show me your muscle'. And he should answer me, 'See my dumb-bells'. Your dumb-bells are your own affair; I want to see the effect of them.

"Take the treatise 'On Choice', and see how thoroughly I have perused it.

---

132   Marcus Aurelius, *Meditations*, IV, II, ibid

I am not asking about this, O slave, but how you act in choosing and refusing, how you manage your desires and aversions, your intentions and purposes, how you meet events -- whether you are in harmony with nature's laws or opposed to them. If in harmony, give me evidence of that, and I will say you are progressing; if the contrary, you may go your way, and not only comment on your books, but write some like them yourself; and what good will it do you?"

Epictetus, *On Choice*[133]

"Indeed the state of all who are preoccupied is wretched, but the most wretched are those who are toiling not even at their own preoccupations, but must regulate their sleep by another's, and their walk by another's pace, and obey orders in those freest of all things, loving and hating. If such people want to know how short their lives are, let them reflect how small a portion is their own."

Seneca, *On Shortness of Life*[134]

"What is your art? To be good. And how is this accomplished well except by general principles, some about the nature of the universe, and others about the proper constitution of man?"

---

133 Epictetus, *On Choice*
134 Seneca, *On Shortness of Life*

Marcus Aurelius, *Meditations*

"Since it's clear then that what sets itself in motion is eternal, who could fail to attribute such a nature to the soul. Anything set in motion by external impetus is inanimate; what is animate moves by its own interior impulse. This is the nature and power of soul. And because it is the one thing out of all that sets itself in motion, then surely it was never born and will last forever."

Cicero, *On Living and Dying Well*[135]

"But when you are looking on anyone as a friend when you do not trust him as you trust yourself, you are making a grave mistake, and have failed to grasp sufficiently the full force of true friendship."

Seneca, *Letters From a Stoic*[136]

"We must stand up against old age and make up for its drawbacks by taking pains. We must fight it as we should an illness. We must look after our health, use moderate exercise, take just enough food and drink to recruit, but not to overload, our strength. Nor is it the body alone that must be supported, but the intellect and soul much more."

---

135   Cicero, *On Living and Dying Well*
136   Seneca, *Letters From a Stoic*, Letter 36

Cicero, *On Old Age*[137]

"And in the case of superior things like stars, we discover a kind of unity in separation. The higher we rise on the scale of being, the easier it is to discern a connection even among things separated by vast distances."

Marcus Aurelius, *Meditations*

"These reasonings are unconnected: 'I am richer than you, therefore I am better'; 'I am more eloquent than you, therefore I am better.' The connection is rather this: 'I am richer than you, therefore my property is greater than yours;' 'I am more eloquent than you, therefore my style is better than yours.' But you, after all, are neither property nor style."

Epictetus, *Enchiridion*

"It is better to do wrong seldom and to own it, and to act right for the most part, than seldom to admit that you have done wrong and to do wrong often."

---

[137] Cicero, *On Old Age*

Epictetus, Enchiridion[138]

"How can life be worth living, to use the words of Ennius, which lacks that repose which is to be found in the mutual good-will of a friend? What can be more delightful than to have some one to whom you can say everything with the same absolute confidence as to yourself? Is not prosperity robbed of half its value if you have no one to share your joy? On the other hand, misfortunes would be hard to bear if there were not some one to feel them even more acutely than yourself."

Cicero, *On Friendship*[139]

"Very little is needed to make a happy life; it is all within yourself in your way of thinking."

Marcus Aurelius, *Meditations*[140]

"If you wish your house to be well managed, imitate the Spartan Lycurgus. For as he did not fence his city with walls, but fortified the inhabitants by virtue and preserved the city always free; so do you not cast around (your house) a large court and raise high towers, but strengthen the dwellers by good-will and fidelity and friendship, and then nothing harmful will enter it, not even if the whole band of wickedness shall array itself against it.

---

138   Epictetus, *Enchiridion*, 18
139   Cicero, *On Friendship*
140   Marcus Aurelius, *Meditations*, IV, III

Epictetus, *Enchiridion*[141]

"I conclude, then, that the plea of having acted in the interests of a friend is not a valid excuse for a wrong action. . . . We may then lay down this rule of friendship--neither ask nor consent to do what is wrong. For the plea "for friendship's sake" is a discreditable one, and not to be admitted for a moment."

Cicero, *On Living Well*[142]

"As for myself, I can only exhort you to look on Friendship as the most valuable of all human possessions, no other being equally suited to the moral nature of man, or so applicable to every state and circumstance, whether of prosperity or adversity, in which he can possibly be placed. But at the same time I lay it down as a fundamental axiom that "true Friendship can only subsist between those who are animated by the strictest principles of honour and virtue." When I say this, I would not be thought to adopt the sentiments of those speculative moralists who pretend that no man can justly be deemed virtuous who is not arrived at that state of absolute perfection which constitutes, according to their ideas, the character of genuine wisdom. This opinion may appear true, perhaps, in theory, but is altogether

---

141   Epictetus, *Enchiridion*, 20
142   Cicero, *On Living Well*

inapplicable to any useful purpose of society, as it supposes a degree of virtue to which no mortal was ever capable of rising."

Cicero, *Letters*[143]

"We are at the mercy of whoever wields authority over the things we either desire or detest. If you would be free, then, do not wish to have, or avoid, things that other people control, because then you must serve as their slave."

Epictetus, *Discourses*[144]

"If it is not right do not do it; if it is not true do not say it."

Marcus Aurelius, *Meditations*[145]

c. **What to do With Work** – Advice concerning heavy workloads and positive reinforcement.

"If you seek tranquility, do less. Or do what's essential – what the logos of a social being requires, and in the requisite way. Which brings a double satisfaction: to do less, better. Because most of what we say and do is not essential. If you can eliminate

---

143 Cicero, *Letters*
144 Epictetus, *Discourses*, III
145 Marcus Aurelius, *Meditations*, II, ibid

it, you'll have more time, and more tranquility. Ask yourself at every moment, 'Is this necessary?'"

Marcus Aurelius, *Meditations*

"For in this Case, we are not to give Credit to the Many, who say, that none ought to be educated but the Free; but rather to the Philosophers, who say, that the Well-educated alone are free."

Epictetus, *Fragments*[146]

"Think of your many years of procrastination; how the gods have repeatedly granted you further periods of grace, of which you have taken no advantage. It is time now to realize the nature of the universe to which you belong, and of that controlling Power whose offspring you are; and to understand that your time has a limit set to it. Use it, then, to advance your enlightenment; or it will be gone, and never in your power again."

Marcus Aurelius, *Meditations*

A key point to bear in mind: The value of attentiveness varies in proportion to its object. You're better off not giving the small things more time than they deserve.

---

146   Epictetus, Fragment

Marcus Aurelius, *Meditations*

"You should rather suppose that those are involved in worthwhile duties who wish to have daily as their closest friends Zeno, Pythagoras, Democritus and all the other high priests of science, and Aristotle and Theophrastus. None of these will be too busy to see you, none of these will not send his visitor away happier and more devoted to himself, none of these will allow anyone to depart empty-handed. They are at home to all mortals by night and by day."

Seneca, *On Shortness of Life*[147]

We should not be so taken up in the search for truth, as to neglect the needful duties of active life; for it is only action that gives a true value and commendation to virtue.

Cicero, *On Old Age*[148]

"You need to avoid certain things in your train of thought: everything random, everything irrelevant. And certainly everything self-important or malicious. You need to get used to winnowing your thoughts, so that if someone says, "What are

---

147 Seneca, *On Shortness of Life*
148 Cicero, *On Old Age*

your thinking about?" you can respond at once (and truthfully) that you are thinking this or thinking that."

Marcus Aurelius, *Meditations*[149]

There is nothing that we can properly call our own but our time, and yet everybody fools us out of it who has a mind to do it. If a man borrows a paltry sum of money, there must needs be bonds and securities, and every common civility is presently charged upon account. But he who has my time thinks he owes me nothing for it, though it be a debt that gratitude itself can never repay.

Seneca, *Letters From a Stoic*[150]

"I have the better right to indulgence herein, because my devotion to letters strengthens my oratorical powers, and these, such as they are, have never failed my friends in their hour of peril. Yet insignificant though these powers may seem to be, I fully realize from what source I draw all that is highest in them. Had I not persuaded myself from my youth up, thanks to the moral lessons derived from a wide reading, that nothing is to be greatly sought after in this life save glory and honor, and that in their quest all bodily pains and all dangers of death or exile

---

149   Marcus Aurelius, *Meditations*, II, XI, III
150   Seneca, *Letters From a Stoic*, Letter 53

should be lightly accounted, I should never have borne for the safety of you all the burnt of many a bitter encounter, or bared my breast to the daily onsets of abandoned persons. All literature, all philosophy, all history, abounds with incentives to noble action, incentives which would be buried in black darkness were the light of the written word not flashed upon them."

Cicero, *On Old Age*[151]

"To be sure, external things of whatever kind require skill in their use, but we must not grow attached to them; whatever they are, they should only serve for us to show how skilled we are in our handling of them."

Marcus Aurelius, *Meditations*

"If you have been placed in a position above others, are you automatically going to behave like a despot? Remember who you are and whom you govern – that they are kinsmen, brothers by nature, fellow descendants of Zeus."

---

151   Cicero, *On Old Age*

Marcus Aurelius, *Meditations*[152]

"If you apply yourself to study you will avoid all boredom with life, you will not long for night because you are sick of daylight, you will be neither a burden to yourself nor useless to others, you will attract many to become your friends and the finest people will flock about you."

Seneca, *Letters From a Stoic*[153]

"Don't just say you have read books. Show that through them you have learned to think better, to be a more discriminating and reflective person. Books are the training weights of the mind. They are very helpful, but it would be a bad mistake to suppose that one has made progress simply by having internalized their contents."

Epictetus, *Discourses*[154]

"Show me one person who cares how they act, someone for whom success is less important than the manner in which it is achieved. While out walking, who gives any thought to the act of walking itself? Who pays attention to the process of planning, not just the outcome?"

---

152   Marcus Aurelius, *Meditations*, V, II, IV
153   Seneca, *Letters From a Stoic,* Letter 21
154   Epictetus, *Discourses*, II

Marcus Aurelius, *Meditations*

"Hour by hour resolve firmly to do what comes to hand with dignity, and with humanity, independence, and justice. Allow your mind freedom from all other considerations. This you can do, if you will approach each action as though it were your last, dismissing the desire to create an impression, the admiration of self, the discontent with your lot. See how little man needs to master, for his days to flow on in quietness and piety: he has but to observe these few counsels, and the gods will ask nothing more."

Marcus Aurelius, *Meditations*[155]

"Though, even if there were no such great advantage to be reaped from it, and if it were only pleasure that is sought from these studies, still I imagine you would consider it a most reasonable and liberal employment of the mind: for other occupations are not suited to every time, nor to every age or place; but these studies are the food of youth, the delight of old age; the ornament of prosperity, the refuge and comfort of adversity; a delight at home, and no hindrance abroad; they are companions by night, and in travel, and in the country."

---

[155] Marcus Aurelius, *Meditations*, II

Cicero, *On Oration*[156]

"To want to know more than is sufficient is a form of intemperance. Apart from which this kind of obsession with the arts turns people into pedantic, irritating, tactless, self-satisfied bores, not learning what they need simply because they spend their time learning things they will never need. The scholar Didymus wrote four thousand works: I should feel sorry him if he had merely read so many useless works."

Seneca, *Letters From a Stoic*

"Tentative efforts lead to tentative outcomes. Therefore, give yourself fully to your endeavors. Decide to construct your character through excellent actions and determine to pay the price of a worthy goal. The trials you encounter will introduce you to your strengths. Remain steadfast...and one day you will build something that endures: something worthy of your potential."

Epictetus, Discourses[157]

"Why do you want to read anyway – for the sake of amusement or mere erudition? Those are poor, fatuous pretexts. Reading

---

156   Cicero, *On Oration*
157   Epictetus, *Discourses, IV*

should serve the goal of attaining peace; if it doesn't make you peaceful, what good is it?"

Epictetus, *Of Human Freedom*

"But only philosophy will wake us; only philosophy will shake us out of that heavy sleep. Devote yourself entirely to her. You're worthy of her, she's worthy of you-fall into each other's arms. Say a firm, plain no to every other occupation."

Seneca, *Letters From a Stoic*[158]

"If, on the other hand, we read books entitled On Impulse not just out of idle curiosity, but in order to exercise impulse correctly; books entitled On Desire and On Aversion so as not to fail to get what we desire or fall victim to what we would rather avoid; and books entitled On Moral Obligation in order to honor our relationships and never do anything that clashes or conflicts with this principle; then we wouldn't get frustrated and grow impatient with our reading.

Instead we would be satisfied to act accordingly. And rather than reckon, as we are used to doing, 'How many lines I read, or wrote, today,' we would pass in review how 'I applied impulse today the way the philosophers recommend"

---

[158] Seneca, *Letters From a Stoic*, Letter 40, Letter 8

Epictetus, *Of Human Freedom*

"We ought, then, to set up images of a kind that can adhere longest in the memory. And we shall do so if we establish likenesses as striking as possible; if we set up images that are not many or vague, but doing something; if we assign to them exceptional beauty or singular ugliness; if we dress some of them with crowns or purple cloaks, for example, so that the likeness may be more distinct to us; or if we somehow disfigure them, as by introducing one stained with blood or soiled with mud or smeared with red paint, so that its form is more striking, or by assigning certain comic effects to our images, for that, too, will ensure our remembering them more readily."

Cicero, *Letters*[159]

"In literature, too, it is not great achievement to memorize what you have read while not formulating an opinion of your own."

Epictetus, *Discourses*[160]

"Finally, everybody agrees that no one pursuit can be successfully followed by a man who is preoccupied with many things—eloquence cannot, nor the liberal studies—since the

---

159   Cicero, *Letters*
160   Epictetus, *Discourses*, IV

mind, when distracted, takes in nothing very deeply, but rejects everything that is, as it were, crammed into it. There is nothing the busy man is less busied with than living: there is nothing that is harder to learn."

Seneca, *Letters From a Stoic*[161]

"Of this last kind of comparisons is that quoted from the elder Cato, who, when asked what was the most profitable thing to be done on an estate, replied, "To feed cattle well." "What second best?" "To feed cattle moderately well." "What third best?" "To feed cattle, though but poorly." "What fourth best?" "To plough the land." And when he who had made these inquiries asked, "What is to be said of making profit by usury?" Cato replied, "What is to be said of making profit by murder?"

Cicero, *On Duties*[162]

d. **Open to Possibilities** – What the Stoics thought about views and anticipation of the future.

"My thought for today is something which I found in Epicurus (yes, I actually make a practice of going over to the enemy's camp – by way of reconnaissance, not as a deserter!). 'A cheerful

---

161 Seneca, *Letters From a Stoic*, Letter 13
162 Cicero, *On Duties*

poverty,' he says, 'is an honorable state.' But if it is cheerful it is not poverty at all. It is not the man who has too little who is poor, but the one who hankers after more. What difference does it make how much there is laid away in a man's safe or in his barns, how many head of stock he grazes or how much capital he puts out at interest, if he is always after what is another's and only counts what he has yet to get, never what he has already. You ask what is the proper limit to a person's wealth? First, having what is essential, and second, having what is enough."

Seneca, *Letters From a Stoic*[163]

"People who are physically ill are unhappy with a doctor who doesn't give them advice, because they think he has given up on them. Shouldn't we feel the same towards a philosopher – and assume that he has given up hope of our ever becoming rational – if he will no longer tell us what we need (but may not like) to hear?"

Marcus Aurelius, *Meditations*[164]

"The best Armour of Old Age is a well spent life preceding it; a Life employed in the Pursuit of useful Knowledge, in honourable Actions and the Practice of Virtue; in which he who labours to

---

163   Seneca, *Letters From a Stoic*, Letter 11
164   Marcus Aurelius, *Meditations*, I, X, IV

improve himself from his Youth, will in Age reap the happiest Fruits of them; not only because these never leave a Man, not even in the extremest Old Age; but because a Conscience bearing Witness that our Life was well-spent, together with the Remembrance of past good Actions, yields an unspeakable Comfort to the Soul"

Cicero, *Letters*[165]

"So when you hear that even life and the like are indifferent, don't become apathetic; and by the same token, when you're advised to care about them, don't become superficial and conceive a passion for externals."

Marcus Aurelius, *Meditation*

"Remember that the divine order is intelligent and fundamentally good. Life is not a series of random, meaningless episodes, but an ordered, elegant whole that follows ultimately comprehensible laws."

Epictetus, *Discourses*[166]

"Pain too is just a scary mask: look under it and you will see. The body sometimes suffers, but relief is never far behind. And if

---

165 Cicero, *Letters*
166 Epictetus, *Discourses*

that isn't good enough for you, the door stands open; otherwise put up with it. The door needs to stay open whatever the circumstances, with the result that our problems disappear."

Marcus Aurelius, *Meditations*

"Do not be whirled about, but in every movement have respect to justice, and on the occasion of every impression maintain the faculty of comprehension or understanding."

Marcus Aurelius, *Meditations*

"From the philosopher Catulus, never to be dismissive of a friend's accusation, even if it seems unreasonable, but to make every effort to restore the relationship to its normal condition."

Marcus Aurelius, *Meditations*

"Set aside a certain number of days, during which you shall be content with the scantiest and cheapest fare, with course and rough dress, saying to yourself the while: 'Is this the condition that I feared?'"

Seneca, *Letters From a Stoic*

"This presumption that you possess knowledge of any use has to be dropped before you approach philosophy – just as if we were enrolling in a school of music or mathematics."

Marcus Aurelius, *Meditations*

"There are two things that must be rooted out in human beings - arrogant opinion and mistrust. Arrogant opinion expects that there is nothing further needed, and mistrust assumes that under the torrent of circumstance there can be no happiness."

Epictetus, *Discourses*[167]

"Once you have rid yourself of the affliction there, though, every change of scene will become a pleasure. You may be banished to the ends of the earth, and yet in whatever outlandish corner of the world you may find yourself stationed, you will find that place, whatever it may be like, a hospitable home. Where you arrive does not matter so much as what sort of person you are when you arrive there."

---

[167] Epictetus, *Discourses*, IV

Seneca, *Letters From a Stoic*[168]

"You might as well get on your knees and pray that your nose won't run. A better idea would be to wipe your nose and forgo the prayer. The point is, isn't there anything God gave you for your present problem?"

Marcus Aurelius, *Meditations*[169]

"Why are we not angry if we are told that we have a headache, and why are we angry if we are told that we reason badly, or choose wrongly?" The reason is that we are quite certain that we have not a headache, or are not lame, but we are not so sure that we make a true choice. So having assurance only because we see with our whole sight, it puts us into suspense and surprise when another with his whole sight sees the opposite, and still more so when a thousand others deride our choice. For we must prefer our own lights to those of so many others, and that is bold and difficult."

Epictetus, *Discourses*

"The day has already begun to lessen. It has shrunk considerably, but yet will still allow a goodly space of time if one

---

[168] Seneca, *Letters From a Stoic*, Letter 35, Letter 6
[169] Marcus Aurelius, *Meditations*, IV, X, ibid, V

rises, so to speak, with the day itself. We are more industrious, and we are better men if we anticipate the day and welcome the dawn;"

Seneca, *Letters From a Stoic*

"Now there are two kinds of hardening, one of the understanding, the other of the sense of shame, when a man is resolved not to assent to what is manifest nor to desist from contradictions. Most of us are afraid of mortification of the body, and would contrive all means to avoid such a thing, but we care not about the soul's mortification. And indeed with regard to the soul, if a man be in such a state as not to apprehend anything, or understand at all, we think that he is in a bad condition; but if the sense of shame and modesty are deadened, this we call even power (or strength)."

Epictetus, *Discourses*[170]

"When, therefore, you see anyone eminent in honors, or power, or in high esteem on any other account, take heed not to be hurried away with the appearance, and to pronounce him happy; for, if the essence of good consists in things in our own control, there will be no room for envy or emulation. But, for

---

[170] Epictetus, *Discourses,* IV, ibid

your part, don't wish to be a general, or a senator, or a consul, but to be free;"

Epictetus, *Enchiridion*[171]

---

[171] Epictetus, *Enchiridion*, 3

III. Beat the Heat with Summer Virtue

a. **Relaxing: Not Just for Kids** – The Stoics on leisure.

"The man who spends his time choosing one resort after another in a hunt for peace and quiet, will in every place he visits find something to prevent him from relaxing."

Marcus Aurelius, *Meditations*[172]

"Nothing, to my way of thinking, is a better proof of a well ordered mind than a man's ability to stop just where he is and pass some time in his own company."

Seneca, *Letters From a Stoic*[173]

"These studies which stimulate the young, divert the old, are an ornament in prosperity and a refuge and comfort in adversity; they delight us at home, are no impediment in public life, keep us company at night, in our travels, and whenever we retire to the country."

---

172   Marcus Aurelius, *Meditations*, V
173   Seneca, *Letters From a Stoic*, Letter 30, Letter 26

Cicero, *Pro Archia*

"At times we ought to drink even to intoxication, not so as to drown, but merely to dip ourselves in wine, for wine washes away troubles and dislodges them from the depths of the mind and acts as a remedy to sorrow as it does to some diseases. The inventor of wine is called Liber, not from the license which he gives to our tongues but because he liberates the mind from the bondage of cares and emancipates it, animates it and renders it more daring in all that it attempts."

Seneca, *Letters From a Stoic*

"If you ever happen to turn your attention to externals, for the pleasure of any one, be assured that you have ruined your scheme of life. Be contented, then, in everything, with being a philosopher; and if you with to seem so likewise to any one, appear so to yourself, and it will suffice you."

Epictetus, *Enchiridion*[174]

"For other forms of relaxation are not so universally suited to all ages, times, and places; but these studies [of literature] sustain youth and entertain old age, they enhance prosperity, and offer a refuge and solace in adversity, they delight us when we are at

---

[174] Epictetus, *Enchiridion*, 14

home without hindering us in the wider world, and are with us at night, when we travel and when we visit the countryside."

Cicero, *Pro Archia*[175]

"Cling, therefore, to this sound and wholesome plan of life; indulge the body just so far as suffices for good health. ... Your food should appease your hunger, your drink quench your thirst, your clothing keep out the cold, your house be a protection against inclement weather. It makes no difference whether it is built of turf or variegated marble imported from another country: what you have to understand is that thatch makes a person just as good a roof as gold."

Seneca, *Letters From a Stoic*[176]

"We must consider what is the time for singing, what the time for play, and in whose presence: what will be unsuited to the occasion; whether our companions are to despise us, or we to despise ourselves: when to jest, and whom to mock at: and on what occasion to be conciliatory and to whom: in a word, how one ought to maintain one's character in society. Wherever you swerve from any of these principles, you suffer loss at once; not loss from without, but issuing from the very act itself."

---

175   Cicero, *Pro Archia*
176   Seneca, *Letters From a Stoic,* Letter 21, Letter 35

Epictetus, *Discourses*[177]

"We must go for walks out of doors, so that the mind can be strengthened and invigorated by a clear sky and plenty of fresh air. At times it will acquire fresh energy from a journey by carriage and a change of scene, or from socializing and drinking freely. Occasionally we should even come to the point of intoxication, sinking into drink but not being totally flooded by it; for it does wash away cares, and stirs the mind to its depths, and heals sorrow just as it heals certain diseases."

Seneca, *Letters From a Stoic*

"Let us assume that entertainment is the sole end of reading; even so I think you would hold that no mental employment is so broadening to the sympathies or so enlightening to the understanding. Other pursuits belong not to all times, all ages, all conditions; but this gives stimulus to our youth and diversion to our old age; this adds a charm to success, and offers a haven of consolation to failure. Through the night-watches, on all our journeys, and in our hours of ease, it is our unfailing companion."

---

[177] Epictetus, *Discourses*, III

Cicero, *Letters*[178]

"True happiness is to enjoy the present, without anxious dependence upon the future, not to amuse ourselves with either hopes or fears but to rest satisfied with what we have, which is sufficient, for he that is so wants nothing. The greatest blessings of mankind are within us and within our reach. A wise man is content with his lot, whatever it may be, without wishing for what he has not."

Seneca, *Letters From a Stoic*

b. **On Temperament and Temperature** – Stoic advice on environmental and physical stress.

"Indulge the body just so far as suffices for good health. It needs to be treated somewhat strictly to prevent it from being disobedient to the spirit. Your food should appease your hunger, your drink quench your thirst, your clothing keep out the cold, your house be a protection against inclement weather."

---

178   Cicero, *Letters*

Seneca, *Letters From a Stoic*[179]

"Objective judgment, now, at this very moment. Unselfish action, now, at this very moment. Willing acceptance—now, at this very moment—of all external events. That's all you need."

Marcus Aurelius, *Meditations*[180]

"Everywhere means nowhere. When a person spends all his time in foreign travel, he ends by having many acquaintances, but no friends. And the same thing must hold true of men who seek intimate acquaintance with no single author, but visit them all in a hasty and hurried manner. 3. Food does no good and is not assimilated into the body if it leaves the stomach as soon as it is eaten; nothing hinders a cure so much as frequent change of medicine; no wound will heal when one salve is tried after another; a plant which is often moved can never grow strong. There is nothing so efficacious that it can be helpful while it is being shifted about. And in reading of many books is distraction."

---

179 Seneca, *Letters From a Stoic*, Letter 18, Letter 6
180 Marcus Aurelius, *Meditations*, X

Seneca, *Shortness of Life*

"What good are gilded rooms or precious stones-fitted on the floor, inlaid in the walls, carried from great distances at the greatest expense? These things are pointless and unnecessary- without them isn't it possible to live healthy? Aren't they the source of constant trouble? Don't they cost vast sums of money that, through public and private charity, may have benefited many?"

Musonius Rufus, *How To Live*[181]

"Is this all the habit you acquired when you studied philosophy, to look to others and to hope for nothing from yourself and your own acts? Lament therefore and mourn, and when you eat be fearful that you will have nothing to eat to-morrow. Tremble for your wretched slaves, lest they should steal, or run away, or die. Live in this spirit, and never cease to live so, you who never came near philosophy, except in name, and disgraced its principles so far as in you lies, by showing them to be useless and unprofitable to those who take them up."

---

[181] Musonius Rufus, *How To Live*

Epictetus, *Discourses*[182]

"As far as I am concerned, I know that I have lost not wealth but distractions. The body's needs are few: it wants to be free from cold, to banish hunger and thirst with nourishment; if we long for anything more we are exerting ourselves to serve our vices, not our needs."

Seneca, *On Shortness of Life*[183]

"In a sense, people are our proper occupation. Our job is to do them good and put up with them.

But when they obstruct our proper tasks, they become irrelevant to us—like sun, wind, animals. Our actions may be impeded by them, but there can be no impeding our intentionsor our dispositions. Because we can accommodate and adapt. The mind adapts and converts to its own purposes the obstacle to our acting. The impediment to action advances action. What stands in the way becomes the way."

Marcus Aurelius, *Meditations*

"What difference does it make how much is laid away in a man's safe or in his barns, how many head of stock he grazes or how much capital he puts out at interest, if he is always after what is

---

182 Epictetus, *Discourses*, IV
183 Seneca, *On Shortness of Life*, II

another's and only counts what he has yet to get, never what he has already? You ask what is the proper limit to a person's wealth? First, having what is essential, and second, having what is enough."

Seneca, *Letters From a Stoic*[184]

"First to those universal principles I have spoken of: these you must keep at command, and without them neither sleep nor rise, drink nor eat nor deal with men: the principle that no one can control another's will, and that the will alone is the sphere of good and evil."

Epictetus, *Discourses*[185]

"Everyone has the obligation to ponder well his own specific traits of character. He must also regulate them adequately and not wonder whether someone else's traits might suit him better. The more definitely his own a man's character is, the better it fits him."

---

184   Seneca, *Letters From a Stoic*, Letter 28
185   Epictetus, *Discourses*, II

Cicero, *Letters*[186]

"Just as plants receive nourishment for survival, not pleasure-for humans, food is the medicine of life. Therefore it is appropriate for us to eat for living, not pleasure, especially if we want to follow the wise words of Socrates, who said most men live to eat: I eat to live"

Musonius Rufus, *How To Live*[187]

"I am not a 'wise man,' nor . . . shall I ever be. And so require not from me that I should be equal to the best, but that I should be better than the wicked. It is enough for me if every day I reduce the number of my vices, and blame my mistakes."

Seneca, *Letters From a Stoic*[188]

"Retire into thyself. The rational principle which rules has this nature, that it is content with itself when it does what is just, and so secures tranquility."

---

[186] Cicero, *Letters*
[187] Musonius Rufus, *How To Live*
[188] Seneca, *Letters From a Stoic,* Letter 2, Letter 13

Marcus Aurelius, *Meditations*[189]

"Philosophy calls for simple living, not for doing penance, and the simple way of life need not be a crude one."

Seneca, *Letters From a Stoic*

"For as I like a man in whom there is something of the old, so I like a man in whom there is something of the young; and he who follows this maxim, in body will possibly be an old man but he will never be an old man in mind."

Cicero, *On Old Age*[190]

"Don't let your imagination be crushed by life as a whole. Don't try to picture everything bad that could possibly happen. Stick with the situation at hand, and ask, "Why is this so unbearable? Why can't I endure it?" You'll be embarrassed to answer. Then remind yourself that past and future have no power over you. Only the present—and even that can be minimized. Just mark off its limits.

---

[189] Marcus Aurelius, *Meditations*, VIII
[190] Cicero, *On Old Age*

Marcus Aurelius, *Meditations*

"If a person gave your body to any stranger he met on is way, you would certainly be angry. And do you feel no shame in handing over your own mind to be confused and mystified by anyone who happens to verbally attack you?"

Epictetus, *Enchiridion*[191]

"What progress, you ask, have I made? I have begun to be a friend to myself." That was indeed a great benefit; such a person can never be alone. You may be sure that such a man is a friend to all mankind."

Seneca, *Letters From a Stoic*

"If you live in harmony with nature you will never be poor; if you live according what others think, you will never be rich."

Seneca, *Letters From a Stoic*

"Not to waste time on nonsense. Not to be taken in by conjurors and hoodoo artists with their talk about incantations and exorcism and all the rest of it. Not to be obsessed with quail-fighting or other crazes like that."

---

[191] Epictetus, *Enchiridion*

Marcus Aurelius, *Meditations*[192]

"All outdoors may be bedlam, provided there is no disturbance within."

Seneca, *Letters From a Stoic*[193]

"But nothing will help quite so much as just keeping quiet, talking with other people as little as possible, with yourself as much as possible. For conversation has a kind of charm about it, an insinuating and insidious something that elicits secrets from us just like love or liquor. Nobody will keep the things he hears to himself, and nobody will repeat just what he hears and no more. Neither will anyone who has failed to keep a story to himself keep the name of his informant to himself. Every person without exception has someone to whom he confides everything that is confided to himself. Even supposing he puts some guard in his garrulous tongue and is content with a single pair of ears, he will still be the creator of a host of later listeners – such is the way in which what was but a little while before a secret becomes common rumor."

---

192 Marcus Aurelius, *Meditations*, VII
193 Seneca, *Letters From a Stoic*, Letter 22, Letter 10, Letter 31, Letter 3

Seneca, *Letters From a Stoic*

"Kindness is unconquerable, so long as it is without flattery or hypocrisy. For what can the most insolent man do to you, if you contrive to be kind to him, and if you have the chance gently advise and calmly show him what is right...and point this out tactfully and from a universal perspective. But you must not do this with sarcasm or reproach, but lovingly and without anger in your soul."

Marcus Aurelius, *Meditations*[194]

"In truth, Serenus, I have for a long time been silently asking myself to what I should liken such a condition of mind, and I can find nothing that so closely approaches it as the state of those who, after being released from a long and serious illness, are sometimes touched with fits of fever and slight disorders, and, freed from the last traces of them, are nevertheless disquieted with mistrust, and, though now quite well, stretch out their wrist to a physician and complain unjustly of any trace of heat in their body. It is not, Serenus, that these are not quite well in body, but that they are not quite used to being well; just as even a tranquil sea will show some ripple, particularly when it has just subsided after a storm. What you need, therefore, is not any of those harsher measures which we have already left behind, the

---

[194] Marcus Aurelius, *Meditations*, IV, V

necessity of opposing yourself at this point, of being angry with yourself at that, of sternly urging yourself on at another, but that which comes last -confidence in yourself and the belief that you are on the right path, and have not been led astray by the many cross- tracks of those who are roaming in every direction, some of whom are wandering very near the path itself. But what you desire is something great and supreme and very near to being a god - to be unshaken. "

Seneca, *Letters From a Stoic*

"Asia and Europe: tiny corners of the Cosmos. Every sea: a mere drop. Mount Athos: a lump of dirt. The present moment is the smallest point in all eternity. All is microscopic, changeable, disappearing. All things come from that faraway place, either originating directly from that governing part which is common to all, or else following from it as consequences. So even the gaping jaws of the lion, deadly poison, and all harmful things like thorns or an oozing bog are products of that awesome and noble source. Do not imagine these things to be alien to that which you revere, but turn your Reason to the source of all things."

Marcus Aurelius, *Meditations*

"It does good also to take walks out of doors, that our spirits may be raised and refreshed by the open air and fresh breeze: sometimes we gain strength by driving in a carriage, by travel, by change of air, or by social meals and a more generous allowance of wine."

Seneca, *Letters From a Stoic*[195]

"When you run up against someone else's shamelessness, ask yourself this: Is a world without shamelessness possible?

No. Then don't ask the impossible. There have to be shameless people in the world. This is one of them. The same for someone vicious or untrustworthy, or with any other defect. Remembering that the whole world class has to exist will make you more tolerant of its members."

Marcus Aurelius, *Meditations*

"Are you not scorched by the heat? Are you not cramped for room? Have you not to bathe with discomfort? Are you not drenched when it rains? Have you not to endure the clamor and shouting and such annoyances as these? Well, I suppose you set all this over against the splendour of the spectacle and bear it

---

195 Seneca, *Letters From a Stoic*, Letter 22, Letter 16

patiently. What then? have you not received greatness of heart, received courage, received fortitude? What care I, if I am great of heart, for aught that can come to pass? What shall cast me down or disturb me? What shall seem painful? Shall I not use the power to the end for which I received it, instead of moaning and wailing over what comes to pass?"

Epictetus, *Discourses*[196]

"Which is recorded of Socrates, that he was able both to abstain from, and to enjoy, those things which many are too weak to abstain from, and cannot enjoy without excess. But to be strong enough both to bear the one and to be sober in the other is the mark of a man who has a perfect and invincible soul."

Marcus Aurelius, *Meditations*

"All things of the body stream away like a river, all things of the mind are dreams and delusion; life is warfare, and a visit to a strange land; the only lasting fame is oblivion."

---

196   Epictetus, *Discourses,* III

Marcus Aurelius, *Meditations*[197]

"Two distinctive traits especially identify beyond a doubt a strong and dominant character. One trait is contempt for external circumstances, when one is convinced that men ought to respect, to desire, and to pursue only what is moral and right, that men should be subject to nothing, not to another man, not to some disturbing passion, not to Fortune.

The second trait, when your character has the disposition I outlined just now, is to perform the kind of services that are significant and most beneficial; but they should also be services that are a severe challenge, that are filled with ordeals, and that endanger not only your life but also the many comforts that make life attractive.

Of these two traits, all the glory, magnificence, and the advantage, too, let us not forget, are in the second, while the drive and the discipline that make men great are in the former."

Cicero, *De Officiis*[198]

"Is your cucumber bitter? Throw it away. Are there briars in your path? Turn aside. That is enough. Do not go on and say, "Why were things of this sort ever brought into this world?"

---

[197] Marcus Aurelius, *Meditations,* XI, V, II
[198] Cicero, *De Officiis*

neither intolerable nor everlasting - if thou bearest in mind that it has its limits, and if thou addest nothing to it in imagination. Pain is either an evil to the body (then let the body say what it thinks of it!)-or to the soul. But it is in the power of the soul to maintain its own serenity and tranquility. . . ."

Marcus Aurelius, *Meditations*[199]

c. **Living in Your** Prime – How the Stoics viewed those in their prime and what to do with their vigor.

"Remember to act always as if you were at a symposium. When the food or drink comes around, reach out and take some politely; if it passes you by don't try pulling it back. And if it has not reached you yet, don't let your desire run ahead of you, be patient until your turn comes. Adopt a similar attitude with regard to children, wife, wealth and status, and in time, you will be entitled to dine with the gods. Go further and decline these goods even when they are on offer and you will have a share in the gods' power as well as their company. That is how Diogenes, Heraclitus and philosophers like them came to be called, and considered, divine."

---

[199] Marcus Aurelius, *Meditations*, II, I, IX

Epictetus, *Enchiridion*

"Withdraw into yourself, as far as you can. Associate with those who will make a better man of you. Welcome those whom you yourself can improve. The process is mutual; for men learn while they teach."

Seneca, *Letters From a Stoic*[200]

"The first and most important field of philosophy is the application of principles such as "Do not lie." Next come the proofs, such as why we should not lie. The third field supports and articulates the proofs, by asking, for example, "How does this prove it? What exactly is a proof, what is logical inference, what is contradiction, what is truth, what is falsehood?" Thus, the third field is necessary because of the second, and the second because of the first. The most important, though, the one that should occupy most of our time, is the first. But we do just the opposite. We are preoccupied with the third field and give that all our attention, passing the first by altogether. The result is that we lie – but have no difficulty proving why we shouldn't."

---

[200] Seneca, *Letters From a Stoic*, Letter 24

Epictetus, *Enchiridion*[201]

"Reflect on the other social roles you play. If you are a council member, consider what a council member should do. If you are young, what does being young mean, if you are old, what does age imply, if you are a father, what does fatherhood entail? Each of our titles, when reflected upon, suggests the acts appropriate to it."

Marcus Aurelius, *Meditations*

"The name of peace is sweet, and the thing itself is beneficial, but there is a great difference between peace and servitude. Peace is freedom in tranquility, servitude is the worst of all evils, to be resisted not only by war, but even by death."

Cicero, *De Oratore*[202]

"It is not the man who has too little who is poor, but the one who hankers after more."

---

201   Epictetus, *Enchiridion*
202   Cicero, *De Oratore*

Seneca, *Letters From a Stoic*[203]

"If all emotions are common coin, then what is unique to the good man?

To welcome with affection what is sent by fate. Not to stain or disturb the spirit within him with a mess of false beliefs. Instead, to preserve it faithfully, by calmly obeying God – saying nothing untrue, doing nothing unjust. And if the others don't acknowledge it – this life lived in simplicity, humility, cheerfulness – he doesn't resent them for it, and isn't deterred from following the road where it leads: to the end of life. An end to be approached in purity, in serenity, in acceptance, in peaceful unity with what must be."

Marcus Aurelius, *Meditations*[204]

"When a youth was giving himself airs in the Theatre and saying, 'I am wise, for I have conversed with many wise men,' Epictetus replied, 'I too have conversed with many rich men, yet I am not rich!'."

---

[203]   Seneca, *Letters From a Stoic*, Letter 2
[204]   Marcus Aurelius, *Meditations*, IV

Epictetus, *Fragments*[205]

"Take care of this moment. Immerse yourself in its particulars. Respond to this person, this challenge, this deed. Quit the evasions. Stop giving yourself needless trouble. It is time to really live; to fully inhabit the situation you happen to be in now. You are not some disinterested bystander. Participate. Exert yourself."

Epictetus, *Discourses*

"The perfection of moral character consists in this, in passing every day as if it were the last, and in being neither violently excited nor torpid nor playing the hypocrite."

Marcus Aurelius, *Meditations*

"When you do anything from a clear judgment that it ought to be done, never shrink from being seen to do it, even though the world should misunderstand it; for if you are not acting rightly, shun the action itself; if you are, why fear those who wrongly censure you?"

---

[205] Epictetus, Fragment

Enchiridion, *Discourses*[206]

"A man should always have these two rules in readiness. First, to do only what the reason of your ruling and legislating faculties suggest for the service of man. Second, to change your opinion whenever anyone at hand sets you right and unsettles you in an opinion, but this change of opinion should come only because you are persuaded that something is just or to the public advantage, not because it appears pleasant or increases your reputation."

Marcus Aurelius, *Meditations*[207]

"The condition and characteristic of an uninstructed person is this: he never expects from himself profit (advantage) nor harm, but from externals. The condition and characteristic of a philosopher is this: he expects all advantage and all harm from himself."

Epictetus, *Enchiridion*

"Take care not to hurt the ruling faculty of your mind. If you were to guard against this in every action, you should enter upon those actions more safely."

---

206   Enchiridion, *Discourses*, II, ibid
207   Marcus Aurelius, *Meditations*, III

Epictetus, *Enchiridion*[208]

"What can be more delightful than to have some one to whom you can say everything with the same absolute confidence as to yourself? Is not prosperity robbed of half its value if you have no one to share your joy?"

Cicero, *On Old Age*[209]

"For it is dangerous to attach one's self to the crowd in front, and so long as each one of us is more willing to trust another than to judge for himself, we never show any judgement in the matter of living, but always a blind trust, and a mistake that has been passed on from hand to hand finally involves us and works our destruction. It is the example of other people that is our undoing; let us merely separate ourselves from the crowd, and we shall be made whole. But as it is, the populace,, defending its own iniquity, pits itself against reason. And so we see the same thing happening that happens at the elections, where, when the fickle breeze of popular favour has shifted, the very same persons who chose the praetors wonder that those praetors were chosen."

---

208   Epictetus, *Enchiridion*, 12, 22
209   Cicero, *On Old Age*

Seneca, *Letters From a Stoic*[210]

"It is one thing to put bread and wine away in a store-room, and quite another to eat them. What is eaten is digested and distributed around the body, to become sinews, flesh, bones, blood, a good complexion, sound breathing. What is stored away is ready at hand, to be sure, to be taken out and displayed whenever you wish, but you derive no benefit from it, except that of having the reputation of possessing it."

Epictetus, *Discourses*[211]

---

[210] Seneca, *Letters From a Stoic*, Letter 23
[211] Epictetus, *Discourses*, II

IV. Fall, A Time of Change

a. **The Stoics and Loss** – Stoics on dealing with life changes.

"Never let the future disturb you. You will meet it, if you have to, with the same weapons of reason which today arm you against the present."

Marcus Aurelius, *Meditations*

"Until we have begun to go without them, we fail to realize how unnecessary many things are. We've been using them not because we needed them but because we had them."

Seneca, *Letters From a Stoic*[212]

"Human life. Duration: momentary. Nature: changeable. Perception: dim. Condition of Body: decaying. Soul: spinning around. Fortune: unpredictable. Lasting Fame: uncertain. Sum Up: The body and its parts are a river, the soul a dream and mist, life is warfare and a journey far from home, lasting reputation is oblivion."

---

[212] Seneca, *Letters From a Stoic*, Letter 22, Letter 19

Marcus Aurelius, *Meditations*

"Some people will say that memory fades away as the years pass. Of course it does if you don't exercise it or aren't very bright to begin with."

Cicero, *On Old Age*[213]

The gods are not to blame. They do nothing wrong, on purpose or by accident. Nor men either; they don't do it on purpose. No one is to blame.

Marcus Aurelius, *Meditations*[214]

"Remember that all we have is "on loan" from Fortune, which can reclaim it without our permission—indeed, without even advance notice. Thus, we should love all our dear ones, but always with the thought that we have no promise that we may keep them forever—nay, no promise even that we may keep them for long."

Seneca, *Letters From a Stoic*

"And here are two of the most immediately useful thoughts you will dip into. First that things cannot touch the mind: they are

---

213 Cicero, *On Old Age*
214 Marcus Aurelius, *Meditations*, V, IV, I, ibid

external and inert; anxieties can only come from your internal judgment. Second, hat all these things you see will change almost as you look at them, and then will be no more. Constantly bring to mind all that you yourself have already seen changed. The universe is change: life is judgment."

Marcus Aurelius, *Meditations*

"All the greatest blessings are a source of anxiety, and at no time should fortune be less trusted than when it is best; to maintain prosperity there is need of other prosperity, and in behalf of the prayers that have turned out well we must make still other prayers. For everything that comes to us from chance is unstable, and the higher it rises, the more liable it is to fall. Moreover, what is doomed to perish brings pleasure to no one; very wretched, therefore, and not merely short, must the life of those be who work hard to gain what they must work harder to keep. By great toil they attain what they wish, and with anxiety hold what they have attained; meanwhile they take no account of time that will never more return."

Seneca, *Letters From a Stoic*

Time is a sort of river of passing events, and strong is its current; no sooner is a thing brought to sight than it is swept by and another takes its place, and this too will be swept away.

Marcus Aurelius, *Meditations*

"Remember two things: i. that everything has always been the same, and keeps recurring, and it makes no difference whether you see the same things recur in a hundred years or two hundred, or in an infinite period; ii. that the longest-lived and those who will die soonest lose the same thing. The present is all that they can give up, since that is all you have, and what you do not have you cannot lose."

Marcus Aurelius, *Meditations*

"And what's so bad about your being deprived of that?... All things seem unbearable to people who have become spoiled, who have become soft through a life of luxury, ailing more in the mind than they ever are in the body."

Seneca, *Letters From a Stoic*[215]

Remember that you ought to behave in life as you would at a banquet. As something is being passed around it comes to you; stretch out your hand, take a portion of it politely. It passes on; do not detain it. Or it has not come to you yet; do not project your desire to meet it, but wait until it comes in front of you. So

---

215   Seneca, *Letters From a Stoic*, Letter 13, Letter 9

act toward children, so toward a wife, so toward office, so toward wealth."

Epictetus, *Enchiridion*[216]

"In the life of a man, his time is but a moment, his being an incessant flux, his sense a dim rushlight, his body a prey of worms, his soul an unquiet eddy, his fortune dark, his fame doubtful. In short, all that is body is as coursing waters, all that is of the soul as dreams and vapors."

Marcus Aurelius, *Meditations*[217]

"That ever then the poor body of Socrates should have been dragged away and haled by main force to prison! That ever hemlock should have been given to the body of Socrates; that that should have breathed its life away! — Do you marvel at this? Do you hold this unjust? Is it for this that you accuse God? Had Socrates no compensation for this? Where then for him was the ideal Good? Whom shall we hearken to, you or him? And what says he?

"Anytus and Melitus may put me to death: to injure me is beyond their power."

---

216   Epictetus, *Enchiridion*, 18
217   Marcus Aurelius, *Meditations*, X, V, IV

And again:—

"If such be the will of God, so let it be."

Epictetus, *Discourses*[218]

"No one could endure lasting adversity if it continued to have the same force as when it first hit us. We are all tied to Fortune, some by a loose and golden chain, and others by a tight one of baser metal: but what does it matter? We are all held in the same captivity, and those who have bound others are themselves in bonds - unless you think perhaps that the left-hand chain is lighter. One man is bound by high office, another by wealth; good birth weighs down some, and a humble origin others; some bow under the rule of other men and some under their own; some are restricted to one place by exile, others by priesthoods: all life is a servitude.

So you have to get used to your circumstances, complain about them as little as possible, and grasp whatever advantage they have to offer: no condition is so bitter that a stable mind cannot find some consolation in it."

---

218   Epictetus, *Discourses*

Seneca, *Letters From a Stoic*[219]

"Is any man afraid of change? What can take place without change? What then is more pleasing or more suitable to the universal nature? And can you take a hot bath unless the wood for the fire undergoes a change? And can you be nourished unless the food undergoes a change? And can anything else that is useful be accomplished without change? Do you not see then that for yourself also to change is just the same, and equally necessary for the universal nature?"

Marcus Aurelius, *Meditations*

"Just as apples when unripe are torn from trees, but when ripe and mellow drop down, so it is violence that takes life from young men, ripeness from old. This ripeness is so delightful to me that, as I approach nearer to death, I seem, as it were, to be sighting land, and to be coming to port at last after a long voyage."

Cicero, *On Old Age*

"How unlucky I am that this should happen to me. But not at all. Perhaps, say how lucky I am that I am not broken by what has happened, and I am not afraid of what is about to happen. For

---

[219] Seneca, *Letters From a Stoic*

the same blow might have stricken anyone, but not many would have absorbed it without capitulation and complaint."

Marcus Aurelius, *Meditations*

"Everything is only for a day, both that which remembers and that which is remembered.

"Observe constantly that all things take place by change, and accustom thyself to consider that the nature of the universe loves nothing so much as to change things which are and to make new things like them. For everything that exists is in a manner the seed of that which will be."

Marcus Aurelius, *Meditations*

"As I give thought to the matter, I find four causes for the apparent misery of old age; first it withdraws us from active accomplishments; second, it renders the body less powerful; third, it deprives us of almost all forms of enjoyment; fourth, it stands not far from death."

Cicero, *On Old Age*[220]

---

220   Cicero, *On Old Age*

b. **Being Prepared** – Passages on reflecting on and preparing for shifts in fortune.

"Every part of me then will be reduced by change into some part of the universe, and that again will change into another part of the universe, and so on forever."

Marcus Aurelius, *Meditations*

"Perhaps the desire of the thing called fame torments you. See how soon everything is forgotten, and look at the chaos of infinite time on each side of the present, and the emptiness of applause, and the fickleness and lack of judgment in those who pretend to give praise, and the narrowness of its domain, and be quiet at last."

Marcus Aurelius, *Meditations*[221]

"The man who looks for the morrow without worrying over it knows a peaceful independence and a happiness beyond all others. Whoever has said, 'I have lived' receives a windfall every day he gets up in the morning."

---

[221] Marcus Aurelius, *Meditations*, II, I, ibid, IV, XII

Seneca, *Letters From a Stoic*[222]

"Treat what you don't have as nonexistent. Look at what you have, the things you value most, and think of how much you'd crave them if you didn't have them. But be careful. Don't feel such satisfaction that you start to overvalue them – that it would upset you to lose them."

Marcus Aurelius, *Meditations*

"If you want to make progress, put up with being perceived as ignorant or naive in worldly matters, don't aspire to a reputation for sagacity. If you do impress others as somebody, don't altogether believe it. You have to realize, it isn't easy to keep your will in agreement with nature, as well as externals. Caring about the one inevitably means you are going to shortchange the other."

Epictetus, *Discourses*

"Constantly recall those who have complained greatly about anything, those who have been most conspicuous by the greatest fame or misfortunes or enmities or fortunes of any kind: then think, where are they all now? Smoke and ash and a tale, or not even a tale."

---

[222] Seneca, *Letters From a Stoic,* Letter 39

Marcus Aurelius, *Meditations*

"Luck is what happens when preparation meets opportunity."

Seneca, *Letters From a Stoic*

"Keep in mind how fast things pass by and are gone – those that are now and those to come. Existence flows past us like a river: the 'what' is in constant flux, the 'why' has a thousand variations. Nothing is stable, not even what's right here. The infinity of past and future gapes before us – a chasm whose depths we cannot see."

Marcus Aurelius, *Meditations*

"Here is your great soul—the man who has given himself over to Fate; on the other hand, that man is a weakling and a degenerate who struggles and maligns the order of the universe and would rather reform the gods than reform himself."

Seneca, *Letters From a Stoic*[223]

"Think of yourself as dead. You have lived your life. Now, take what's left and live it properly. What doesn't transmit light creates its own darkness."

---

[223] Seneca, *Letters From a Stoic*, Letter 10, Letter 18

Marcus Aurelius, *Meditations*[224]

"None of these things are foretold to me; but either to my paltry body, or property, or reputation, or children, or wife. But to me all omens are lucky, if I will. For whichever of these things happens, it is in my control to derive advantage from it."

Epictetus, *Discourses*[225]

"What would Heracles have been if he had said, "How am I to prevent a big lion from appearing, or a big boar, or brutal men?" What care you, I say? If a big boar appears, you will have a greater struggle to engage in; if evil men appear, you will free the world from evil men."

Epictetus, *Discourses*[226]

"The supreme ideal does not call for any external aids. It is homegrown, wholly self-developed. Once it starts looking outside itself for any part of itself it is on the way to being dominated by fortune."

---

[224] Marcus Aurelius, *Meditations*, X, II, VI
[225] Epictetus, *Discourses*, II, ibid
[226] Epictetus, *Discourses*, II

Seneca, *Letters From a Stoic*

"Thou sayest, Men cannot admire the sharpness of thy wits.- Be it so: but there are many other things of which thou canst not say, I am not formed for them by nature. Show those qualities then which are altogether in thy power, sincerity, gravity, endurance of labour, aversion to pleasure, contentment with thy portion and with few things, benevolence, frankness, no love of superfluity, freedom from trifling magnanimity. Dost thou not see how many qualities thou art immediately able to exhibit, in which there is no excuse of natural incapacity and unfitness, and yet thou still remainest voluntarily below the mark? Or art thou compelled through being defectively furnished by nature to murmur, and to be stingy, and to flatter, and to find fault with thy poor body, and to try to please men, and to make great display, and to be so restless in thy mind? No, by the gods: but thou mightest have been delivered from these things long ago. Only if in truth thou canst be charged with being rather slow and dull of comprehension, thou must exert thyself about this also, not neglecting it nor yet taking pleasure in thy dullness."

Marcus Aurelius, *Meditations*[227]

"Barley porridge, or a crust of barley bread, and water do not make a very cheerful diet, but nothing gives one keener pleasure

---

[227] Marcus Aurelius, *Meditations*, X

than having the ability to derive pleasure even from that-- and the feeling of having arrived at something which one cannot be deprived of by any unjust stroke of fortune."

Seneca, *Letters From a Stoic*[228]

"Seek not for events to happen as you wish but rather wish for events to happen as they do and your life will go smoothly."

Epictetus, *Enchiridion*

"For the only safe harbor in this life's tossing, troubled sea is to refuse to be bothered about what the future will bring and to stand ready and confident, squaring the breast to take without skulking or flinching whatever fortune hurls at us."

Seneca, *Letters From a Stoic*

"Your days are numbered. Use them to throw open the windows of your soul to the sun. If you do not, the sun will soon set, and you with it."

---

228   Seneca, *Letters From a Stoic,* Letter 2, ibid, Letter 60

Marcus Aurelius, *Meditations*

"The greatest obstacle to living is expectancy, which hangs upon tomorrow and loses today. You are arranging what is in Fortune's control and abandoning what lies in yours."

Seneca, *Letters From a Stoic*

"So you wish to conquer in the Olympic Games, my friend? And I, too... But first mark the conditions and the consequences. You will have to put yourself under discipline; to eat by rule, to avoid cakes and sweetmeats; to take exercise at the appointed hour whether you like it or not, in cold and heat; to abstain from cold drinks and wine at your will. Then, in the conflict itself you are likely enough to dislocate your wrist or twist your ankle, to swallow a great deal of dust, to be severely thrashed, and after all of these things, to be defeated."

Epictetus, *Discourses*[229]

"I was once a fortunate man but at some point fortune abandoned me.
But true good fortune is what you make for yourself. Good fortune: good character, good intentions, and good actions."

---

[229]   Epictetus, *Discourses, II*

Marcus Aurelius, *Meditations*[230]

"Neither should a ship rely on one small anchor, nor should life rest on a single hope."

Epictetus, *Enchiridion*[231]

"Count your years and you'll be ashamed to be wanting and working for exactly the same things as you wanted when you were a boy. Of this one thing make sure against your dying day - that your faults die before you do. Have done with those unsettled pleasures, which cost one dear - they do one harm after they're past and gone, not merely when they're in prospect. Even when they're over, pleasures of a depraved nature are apt to carry feelings of dissatisfaction, in the same way as a criminal's anxiety doesn't end with the commission of the crime, even if it's undetected at the time. Such pleasures are insubstantial and unreliable; even if they don't do one any harm, they're fleeting in character. Look around for some enduring good instead. And nothing answers this description except what the spirit discovers for itself within itself. A good character is the only guarantee of everlasting, carefree happiness. Even if some obstacle to this comes on the scene, its appearance is only to be compared to that

---

230 Marcus Aurelius, *Meditations*, I, ibid
231 Epictetus, *Enchiridion*, 13

of clouds which drift in front of the sun without ever defeating its light."

Seneca, *Letters From a Stoic*[232]

"Another thing which will help you is to turn your mind to other thoughts and that way get away from your suffering. Call to mind things which you have done that have been upright or courageous; run over in your mind the finest parts you have played."

Marcus Aurelius, *Meditations*

"Never let the future disturb you. You will meet it, if you have to, with the same weapons of reason which today arm you against the present."

Marcus Aurelius, *Meditations*

"For I am not Eternity, but a human being — a part of the whole, as an hour is part of the day. I must come like the hour, and like the hour must pass!"

---

[232] Seneca, *Letters From a Stoic*, Letter 16, Letter 31

Epictetus, *Discourses* [233]

"It is always our choice whether or not we wish to pay the price for life's rewards. And often it is best for us not to pay the price, for the price might be our integrity."

Epictetus, *Fragments*

"Look back over the past, with its changing empires that rose and fell, and you can foresee the future too."

Marcus Aurelius, *Meditations* [234]

"Each day acquire something that will fortify you against poverty, against death, indeed against other misfortunes as well; and after you have run over many thoughts, select one to be thoroughly digested that day."

Seneca, *Letters From a Stoic* [235]

c. **Dealing with Death** – The Stoics and death, personal and impersonal.

---

[233] Epictetus, *Discourses*, III
[234] Marcus Aurelius, *Meditations*, II, IV, II
[235] Seneca, *Letters From a Stoic*, Letter 12

"It is more necessary for the soul to be cured than the body; for it is better to die than to live badly."

Epictetus, *Fragments*[236]

"The gods either have power or they have not. If they have not, why pray to them? If they have, then instead of praying to be granted or spared such-and-such a thing, why not rather pray to be delivered from dreading it, or lusting for it, or grieving over it? Clearly, if they can help a man at all, they can help him in this way. You will say, perhaps, 'But all that is something they have put in my own power.' Then surely it were better to use your power and be a free man, than to hanker like a slave and a beggar for something that is not in your power. Besides, who told you the gods never lend their aid even towards things that do lie in our own power? Begin praying in this way, and you will see. Where another man prays 'Grant that I may possess this woman,' let your own prayer be, 'Grant that I may not lust to possess her.' Where he prays, 'Grant me to be rid of such-and-such a one,' you pray, 'Take from me my desire to be rid of him.' Where he begs, 'Spare me the loss of my precious child,' beg rather to be delivered from the terror of losing him. In short, give your petitions a turn in this direction, and see what comes."

---

[236] Epictetus, Fragment

Marcus Aurelius, *Meditations*

"It is our attitude toward events, not events themselves, which we can control. Nothing is by its own nature calamitous -- even death is terrible only if we fear it."

Epictetus, *Enchiridion*

"Finally, waiting for death with a cheerful mind, as being nothing else than a dissolution of the elements of which every living being is compounded. But if there is no harm to the elements themselves in each continually changing into another, why should a man have any apprehension about the change and dissolution of all the elements?"

Marcus Aurelius, *Meditations*[237]

"Men are disturbed not by things, but by the views which they take of things. Thus death is nothing terrible, else it would have appeared so to Socrates. But the terror consists in our notion of death, that it is terrible. When, therefore, we are hindered, or disturbed, or grieved let us never impute it to others, but to ourselves; that is, to our own views. It is the action of an uninstructed person to reproach others for his own misfortunes;

---

[237] Marcus Aurelius, *Meditations*, IX, II, VII

of one entering upon instruction, to reproach himself; and of one perfectly instructed, to reproach neither others or himself."

Epictetus, Enchiridion[238]

"For it is not death or pain that is to be feared, but the fear of pain or death."

Epictetus, *Fragments*

"That which has died falls not out of the universe. If it stays here, it also changes here, and is dissolved into its proper parts, which are elements of the universe and of thyself. And these too change, and they murmur not"."

Marcus Aurelius, *Meditations*

"Death is a release from the impressions of the senses, and from desires that make us their puppets, and from the vagaries of the mind, and from the hard service of the flesh."

Marcus Aurelius, *Meditations*

"What man can you show me who places any value on his time, who reckons the worth of each day, who understands that he is dying daily? For we are mistaken when we look forward to

---

[238] Epictetus, *Enchiridion*, 10

death; the major portion of death has already passed. Whatever years be behind us are in death's hands."

Seneca, *Letters From a Stoic*[239]

"[Do not get too attached to life] for it is like a sailor's leave on the shore and at any time, the captain may sound the horn, calling you back to eternal darkness."

Epictetus, *Discourses*[240]

"A certain Spartan, whose name hasn't even been passed down, despised death so greatly that when he was being led to execution after his condemnation by the ephors, he maintained a relaxed and joyous expression. To an enemy's challenge – 'Is this how you mock the laws of Lycurgus?' – he answered, 'On the contrary, I give great thanks to him, for he decreed a punishment that I can pay without taking out a loan or juggling debts.' O worthy man of Sparta! His spirit was so great that it seems he must have been an innocent man condemned to die. There have been many such in our own country."

---

239   Seneca, *Letters From a Stoic*, Letter 51
240   Epictetus, *Discourses*, III

Cicero, *On Living and Dying Well*[241]

"Wherefore it is a shame for man to begin and to leave off where the brutes do. Rather he should begin there, and leave off where Nature leaves off in us: and that is at contemplation, and understanding, and a manner of life that is in harmony with herself. See then that you do not die without being spectators of these things."

Epictetus, *Enchiridion*[242]

"Just that you do the right thing. The rest doesn't matter. Cold or warm. Tired or well-rested. Despised or honored. Dying...or busy with other assignments. Because dying, too, is one of our assignments in life. There as well: "To do what needs doing." Look inward. Don't let the true nature of anything elude you. Before long, all existing things will be transformed, to rise like smoke (assuming all things become one), or be dispersed in fragments...to move from one unselfish act to another with God in mind. Only there, delight and stillness...when jarred, unavoidably, by circumstances, revert at once to yourself, and don't lose the rhythm more than you can help. You'll have a better grasp of the harmony if you keep going back to it."

---

[241] Cicero, *On Living and Dying Well*
[242] Epictetus, *Enchiridion*, 24

Marcus Aurelius, *Meditations*[243]

"If you shall be afraid not because you must some time cease to live, but if you shall fear never to have begun to live according to nature – then you will be a man worthy of the universe that has produced you, and you will cease to be a stranger in your native land."

Marcus Aurelius, *Meditations*

"It is possible to learn the will of nature from the things in which we do not differ from each other. For example, when someone else's little slave boy breaks his cup we are ready to say, "It's one of those things that just happen." Certainly, then, when your own cup is broken you should be just the way you were when the other person's was broken. Transfer the same idea to larger matters. Someone else's child is dead, or his wife. There is no one would not say, "It's the lot of a human being." But when one's own dies, immediately it is, "Alas! Poor me!" But we should have remembered how we feel when we hear of the same thing about others."

---

243   Marcus Aurelius, *Meditations*, X, ibid

Epictetus, *Enchiridion*[244]

"Do not act as if you were going to live ten thousand years. Death hangs over you. While you live, while it is in your power, be good."

Marcus Aurelius, *Meditations*

"Did not he, then, who, if he had died at that time, would have died in all his glory, owe all the great and terrible misfortunes into which he subsequently fell to the prolongation of his life at that time?"

Cicero, *On Old Age*[245]

"People are delighted to accept pensions and gratuities, for which they hire out their labour or their support or their services. But nobody works out the value of time: men use it lavishly as if it cost nothing. But if death threatens these same people, you will see them praying to their doctors; if they are in fear of capital punishment, you will see them prepared to spend their all to stay alive."

---

244 Epictetus, *Enchiridion*
245 Cicero, *On Old Age*

Seneca, *On The Shortness of Life*[246]

"Brief is man's life and small the nook of the earth where he lives; brief, too, is the longest posthumous fame, buoyed only by a succession of poor human beings who will very soon die and who know little of themselves, much less of someone who died long ago."

Marcus Aurelius, *Meditations*[247]

"What is death? A "tragic mask." Turn it and examine it. See, it does not bite. The poor body must be separated from the spirit either now or later, as it was separated from it before. Why, then, are you troubled, if it be separated now? for if it is not separated now, it will be separated afterward. Why? That the period of the universe may be completed, for it has need of the present, and of the future, and of the past. What is pain? A mask. Turn it and examine it. The poor flesh is moved roughly, then, on the contrary, smoothly. If this does not satisfy you, the door is open: if it does, bear. For the door ought to be open for all occasions; and so we have no trouble."

Epictetus, *Discourses*[248]

---

246 Seneca, *On The Shortness of Life*
247 Marcus Aurelius, *Meditations*, II, IV
248 Epictetus, *Discourses*, III

"Don't let yourself forget how many doctors have died, furrowing their brows over how many deathbeds. How many astrologers, after pompous forecasts about others' ends. How many philosophers, after endless disquisitions on death and immortality. How many warriors, after inflicting thousands of casualties themselves. How many tyrants, after abusing the power of life and death atrociously, as if they were themselves immortal.

How many whole cities have met their end: Helike, Pompeii, Herculaneum, and countless others.

And all the ones you know yourself, one after another. One who laid out another for burial, and was buried himself, and then the man who buried him - all in the same short space of time.

In short, know this: Human lives are brief and trivial. Yesterday a blob of semen; tomorrow embalming fluid, ash.

To pass through this brief life as nature demands. To give it up without complaint.

Like an olive that ripens and falls.

Praising its mother, thanking the tree it grew on."

Marcus Aurelius, *Meditations*[249]

"It is not that we have so little time but that we lose so much. ... The life we receive is not short but we make it so; we are not ill provided but use what we have wastefully."

Seneca, *On The Shortness of Life*[250]

"The history of your life is now complete and your service is ended: and how many beautiful things you have seen; and how many pleasures and pains you have despised; and how many things called honorable you have spurned; and to how many ill-minded folks you have shown a kind disposition."

Marcus Aurelius, *Meditations*[251]

---

249   Marcus Aurelius, *Meditations*
250   Seneca, *On The Shortness of Life*
251   Marcus Aurelius, *Meditations*, IV, V

Bibliography

Epictetus. *The Enchiridion*. Translated by Elizabeth Carter. http://classics.mit.edu/Epictetus/epicench.html.

Aurelius, Marcus. *Meditations*. Translated by George Long. http://classics.mit.edu/Antoninus/meditations.html.

Cicero, Marcus. *On Old Age*. Translated by Robert Allison, 1916. *Internet Archive*, archive.org/stream/cu31924026475230/cu31924026475230_djvu.txt.

Cicero, Marcus T. *On Duties*. Translated by Cyrus R. Edmonds. New York, NY: Harper & Brothers, 1855. https://archive.org/stream/cicerosthreebook00cicerich/cicerosthreebook00cicerich_djvu.txt.

Epictetus. *Discourses*. http://classics.mit.edu/Epictetus/discourses.html.

Seneca, Lucius. *On the Shortness of Life: Life Is Long If You Know How to Use It (Penguin Great Ideas)*. Translated by C.D.N. Costa, 1st ed., Penguin Classics.

Seneca, Lucius. *Letters from a Stoic (Penguin Classics)*. Translated by Robin Campbell, Penguin Classics, 1969.

www.ingramcontent.com/pod-product-compliance
Lightning Source LLC
Chambersburg PA
CBHW071604080526
44588CB00010B/1011